50 COM[I]... ...[S]
FOR VEGAN KIDS

SOLOMON TADLOCK

Copyright © 2021
Solomon Tadlock
50 Comebacks for Vegan Kids
Comebacks For Vegan Kids
All rights reserved.

No part of this publication may be reproduced, distributed, or transmitted in any form or by any means, including photocopying, recording, or other electronic or mechanical methods, without the prior written permission of the publisher, except in the case of brief quotations embodied in critical reviews and certain other non-commercial uses permitted by copyright law.

Solomon Tadlock
Published by Express Results, LLC Austin, TX

Printed in the United States of America
First Printing 2021
First Edition 2021
ISBN: 9798463931115

Important Legal Notice And Disclaimer:

This publication is intended to provide educational information with regard to the subject matter covered.

The reader of this course assumes all responsibility for the use of these materials and information Solomon Tadlock and Express Results LLC assume no responsibility or liability whatsoever on behalf of any purchaser or reader of these materials.

The methodology, training, products, mentoring, or other teaching does not guarantee success and the results may vary.

TABLE OF CONTENTS

Foreword By Robert Cheeke 6

Introduction 10

1. Aren't plants living just like animals? You're killing plants! .14

2. Humans are supposed to be at the top of the food chain and eat meat from other animals (or something like that)....16

3. I saw that meat has B12 and vegetables don't, so that means you need meat to be healthy! 18

4. Humans evolved to eat meat. 20

5. If we aren't supposed to eat meat, why do we have sharp teeth?..22

6. Our ape ancestors ate meat. 24

7. I heard that (insert stupid diet here) also works for getting healthy! 26

8. But being vegan isn't healthy. 28

9. The Big One: where do you get your protein?.....................30

10. But meat gives you more protein so it's better...................32

11. You need meat to be strong. 34

12. Milk gives calcium and you don't drink milk, so you are calcium deficient..36

13. I only eat range-free chickens and eggs. 38

14. Ok if meat is bad, I'll be vegetarian. 40

15. But if we didn't eat them, animals would take over...........42

16. What about if I'm somewhere cold during the winter, where no plants can grow? 44

17. But I could never give up bacon. 46

18. But vegetables are gross..48

19. You care more about animal suffering than human suffering. 50

20. Just one person won't make a difference.........................52

21. I throw fish back when I go fishing. 54

22. But humans are superior..56

23. But humans are smarter, don't we deserve control............58

24. But humans are carnivores..60

25. How come you're skinny (only answer if you're skinny)...62

26. God put animals here to eat...64

27. But the dairy industry doesn't kill cows............................66

28. But people will lose their jobs if we stop eating meat........68

29. Eating animals is completely legal, so it's obviously not wrong. 70

30. But we can kill animals without pain, it's quick so they won't suffer. 72

31. What I eat is a personal choice. 74

32. Vegans are so judgmental...76

33. How about you focus on more important issues. 78

34. Medication you take is tested on animals........................80

35. Veganism is expensive..82

36. Where do you get vitamin D? 84

37. But I would never hurt an animal, I'm making use of already dead animals. 86

38. Lions can eat meat, then what's stopping us? 88

39. Killing them humanely is okay. 90

40. What about eggs? Eggs are fine. 92

41. You can't be 100% vegan. 94

42. But I don't want to change, I am the way I am. 96

43. But I saw on YouTube that the oldest living person eats eggs and bacon for breakfast. 98

44. Being vegan is too much of a commitment. 100

45. Don't give me that crap, I could never give up meat. 102

46. Vegan food makes you fart. 104

47. I heard vegans (insert stupid lie here). 106

48. But meat tastes so good! 108

49. Milk is so good! Why don't you drink it? 110

50. I'm a carnivore! 112

Message To The Reader 114

Citations 115

FOREWORD
BY ROBERT CHEEKE

As someone who has been vegan since I was a teenager (and now I'm in my forties), I have spent decades defending my ethical vegan positions on myriad topics related to morality, health, fitness, and the environment. It wasn't always easy, and if I had a book about vegan comebacks along my vegan journey back then, it would have been easier to communicate my thoughts about veganism when being questioned by others.

Most of us don't like confrontation, and we certainly don't like being teased or bullied simply for being different, or for following a lifestyle that hasn't made it's way into mainstream consciousness yet, and this book will help you find ease and comfort explaining your vegan viewpoints when your vegan lifestyle is called into question.

As Solomon says, "The best way to help animals and the planet is to be kind to others." He goes on to add, "It's kindness that leads to conversations and open minds." I believe that kindness is fundamentally important when trying to move a conversation forward, and dive deeper into that conversation to help each person understand "why" they do what they do, and eat what they eat.

Habits are formed by repeat behavior, and as Solomon points out, it's not always the best behavior that becomes habit, in fact, many poor decisions become addictions, including our addictions to eating animals. In my more than twenty-five years as a vegan, I don't think I've heard anyone put it this way until Solomon explained it in this book, "Most people think that meat is the best source of protein, but in reality, meat is the biggest source of heart attacks." Let that marinate for a minute.

Solomon has all the references and citations to back up the claim in that comeback about protein (which is probably the topic you will get questioned about the most as a vegan).

As you read the 50 comebacks, you will start to see a pattern of logic that ties everything together.

Think about this for a moment. As a society, we're so worried about how we'll get enough protein in our diets, to the point that we obsess about protein consumption, and often look to animal protein to reach our protein needs. But as Solomon points out, the strongest, largest, and longest-lived animals on the planet are all herbivores. The gorilla, the elephant, and the tortoise, respectively, but additional herbivorous powerhouses include rhinos, hippos, bison, rams, and stallions. They all build incredible strength, muscle, and power by eating plants. And you can too.

Furthermore, the plant-based diet and vegan lifestyle extends to human strength and athletic performance as well. Many Olympic medalists, world champions, world record holders, and professional athletes follow a vegan lifestyle (and Solomon mentions a couple of them in the book for reference). But it's not just athletes who are experiencing the benefits of a vegan lifestyle.

Vegans come from all walks of life, from doctors to teachers, to businessmen and businesswomen, to firefighters and volunteers, to entrepreneurs and farmers, to kids and families, and they come from every demographic you can think of. Compassion knows no borders or limitations, and people from around the globe are drawn to a compassionate vegan lifestyle for all the reasons Solomon outlines in his 50 comebacks for vegan kids.

Prepare to be equipped with witty comebacks for those times when people ask you about your protein intake as a vegan or why lions eating meat makes a case for humans to eat meat too. You'll have the confidence and guidance to steer the conversation with kindness while doing a little bit of vegan education and advocacy along the way.

Thank you, Solomon, for having the courage to write a book that will no doubt help others feel more comfortable in conversations and confrontations about veganism, empowering readers to stand up for their beliefs, which is one of the greatest demonstrations of strength anyone can showcase.

– Robert Cheeke, New York Times Bestselling Author
of *The Plant-Based Athlete*

INTRODUCTION

Dear Reader,

Like anyone who is different in any way, you might get bullied or made fun of for being vegan. Being vegan is one of those things that makes people targets. I myself have been made fun of for being vegan, but I always have a comeback ready. I wrote this book so you too can have a comeback in store for the next time someone wants to mess with you for living compassionately and eating a plant-based diet.

My parents are popular vegans that you may have heard of. My Mom, Dr. Brooke Goldner, healed herself from lupus with a healthy vegan diet. She was told that she could never have children, but obviously, that was incorrect due to my existence.

My Dad, Thomas Tadlock, is an exercise scientist who discovered building muscle was easier and faster on a vegan diet.

Believe it or not, I am actually a regular kid. People think that vegans are so weird and stuff, but I am pretty normal. I like to Yo-Yo as a hobby, and I also play the electric guitar. I really, really, really, really, like Minecraft, and I one day want to be a Disney Pixar animator.

If you got this book as a gift or begged your parents to buy this, I just want to say, that you will not regret getting this. I have seen the kind of teasing that kids can do to others. Having a good comeback can make people get off your case and shut up, or you can use these to help shift the focus of the conversation from your diet to more interesting topics.

My hope is that the comeback opens up the conversations with your friends, and I added a discussion under each comeback for you to share more information if you find some open-minded friends.

The most important thing to know, is that kids will always find something to make fun of, and being vegan might just be an easy subject for them to pounce on, but never let it get you down!

I love being vegan; I love being kind to animals, I love taking better care of the Earth, and I love living a healthier life with my family. Kids that aren't vegan are missing out. So, keep doing the right thing, and have your comebacks ready!

Solomon Tadlock

Dedicated to my mom and dad who always give me the best food and advice, to my brother who always has a hug and a joke for me, and to all the future vegan leaders out there who want to join me in making the world a kinder healthier place.

1

Attack:

Aren't plants living just like animals? You're killing plants!

Comeback:

Yes, plants are alive, but do they grow back? Yes. Do they have a nervous system? No. You should have paid more attention in science class.

Explanation:

Since plants do not have pain receptors, nerves, or a brain, they are not conscious, and they do not feel pain. Animals, on the other hand, are conscious, have feelings, and feel love, fear, and pain just like us.[1]

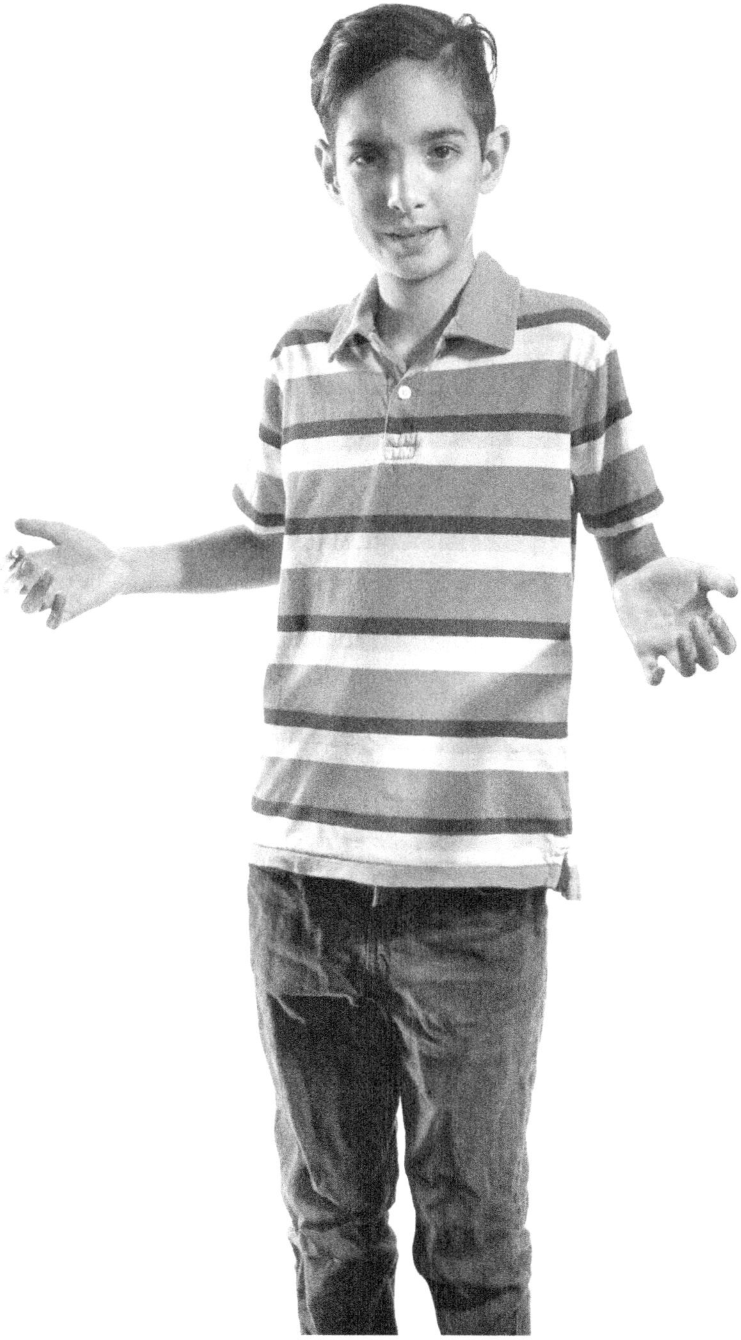

2

Attack:

Humans are supposed to be at the top of the food chain and eat meat from other animals (or something like that).

Comeback:

If we are supposed to eat meat, then why does meat cause cancer?

Explanation:

All animals, including humans, thrive eating their optimal diet and get sick when they eat the wrong diet. The World Health Organization, where scientists from all over the world go to agree on the science, has declared that meats are carcinogens for humans, meaning they cause cancer.[1] That means meat is not the right food for humans. As for being at the top of the food chain, that is a myth! We have figured out a way not to be hunted anymore, but that doesn't mean we are at the top of the food chain or that we are meant to eat animals.[2]

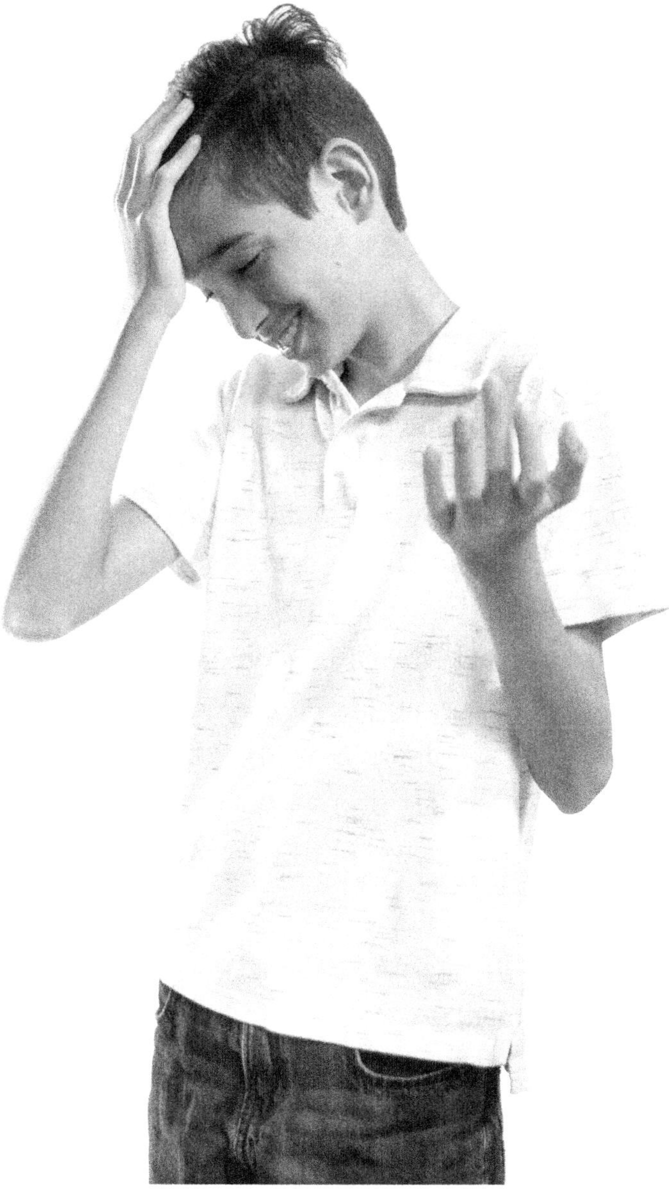

3

Attack:

I saw that meat has B12 and vegetables don't, so that means you need meat to be healthy!

Comeback:

B12 doesn't come from meat, it comes from bacteria in poop! Vegans are on a no-poop diet.

Explanation:

B12 is produced by bacteria that live in the intestines of animals.[4] In nature, when an animal stops to eat from a plant, he will fertilize that plant by pooping on it. Then when a person eats that plant, they will get some B12 from the poop left behind. Now that we wash our vegetables so well, we don't get our B12 that way anymore, and we get our B12 from nutritional yeast or supplements rather than animal poop. Meat is contaminated with poop from when the animal is killed, so meat-eaters tend to eat more poop.[5] Yuck, pass the vitamins!

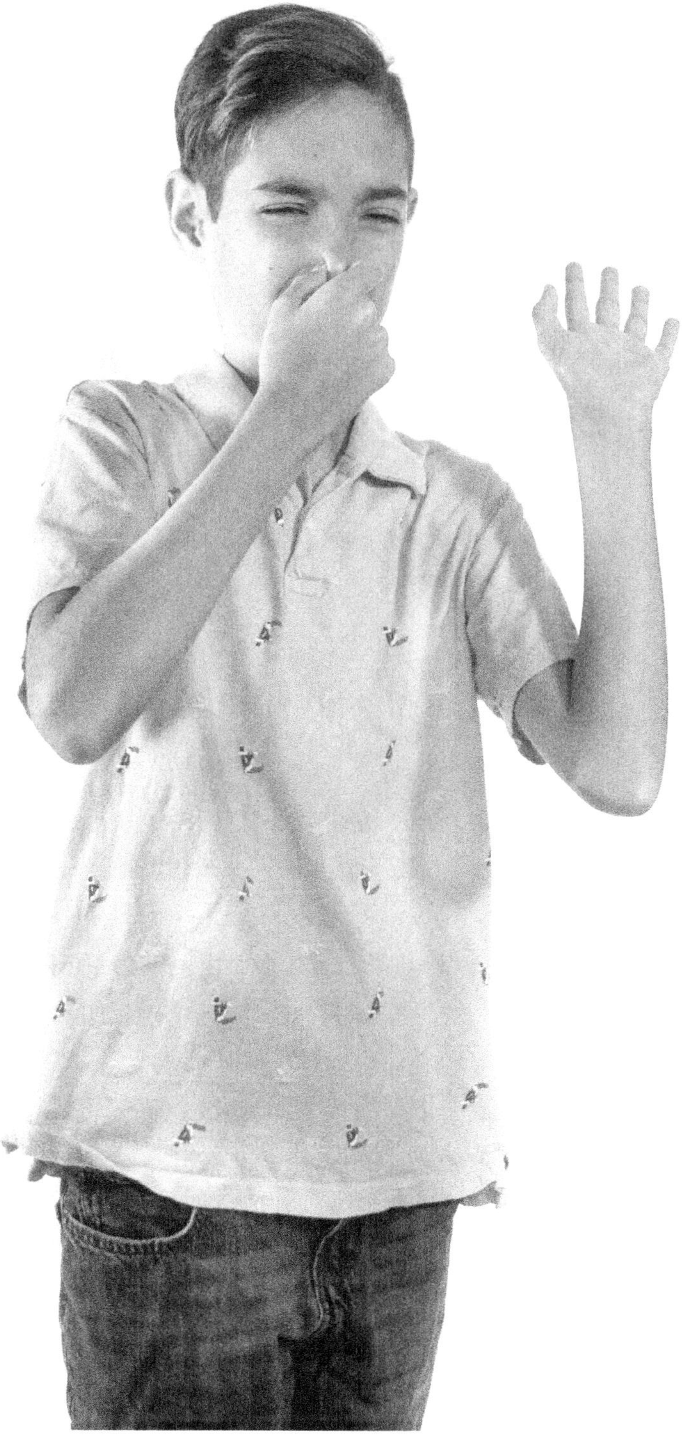

4

Attack:

Humans evolved to eat meat.

Comeback:

Hmm, so we evolved to develop autoimmune disease, heart disease, and cancer from our diet?

Explanation:

Humans are not carnivores, and we did not evolve to eat meat.

Research indicates that our paleolithic ancestors were almost entirely vegetarian.[6]

Before we had supermarkets as we do now, people lived off plants growing from the Earth. In some areas, when it was winter, enough food wouldn't grow, so people ate some meat to survive. They most likely didn't hunt much, but rather scavenged meat left behind by carnivorous predators[6]. Since they only ate small amounts of meat, it didn't cause the diseases we see in people who eat meat every day. Nowadays, we no longer have to eat meat to survive the winter and we are healthier without it.

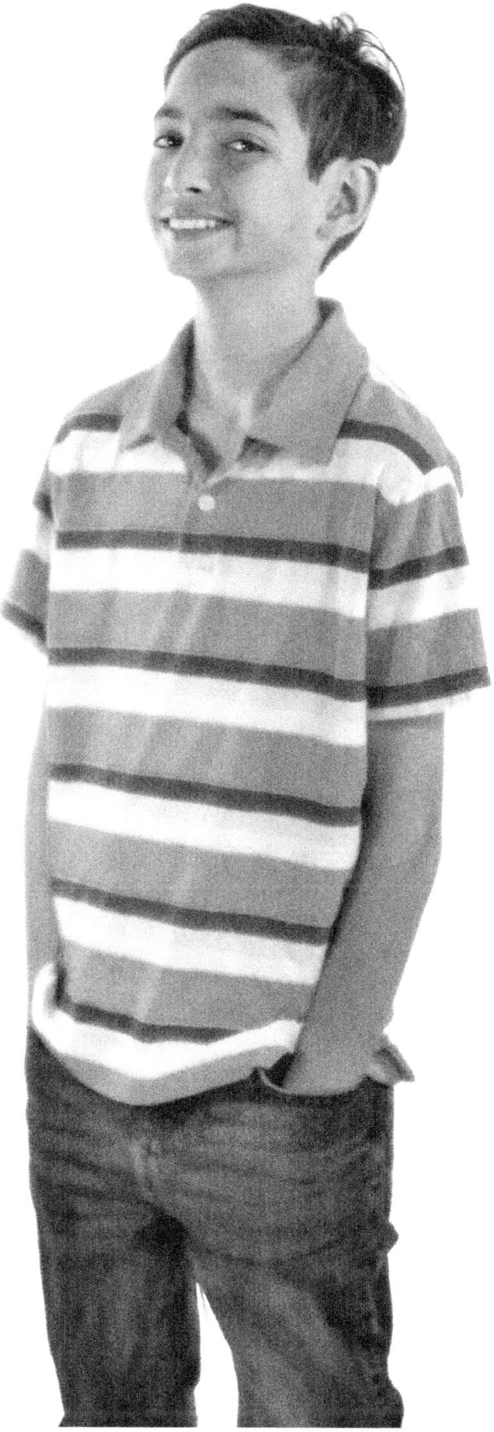

5

Attack:

If we aren't supposed to eat meat, why do we have sharp teeth?

Comeback:

Do you think your little canine teeth can rip an animal's body apart like a lion (insert laughter here)? By the way, even herbivores have sharp canines for self-defense.

Explanation:

Our canine teeth are built for self-defense rather than tearing. Most mammals, including herbivores, have sharp canine teeth.[8] The largest canine teeth of any land animal belong to an herbivore, the hippopotamus.[9] Their canine teeth can grow up to a meter long and are used only for fighting, not eating.[9] They only eat grasses. [7]

23

6

Attack:

Our ape ancestors ate meat.

Comeback:

You are right, while apes are mostly vegan, they also ate bugs. Want some tasty, crunchy bugs?

Explanation:

It may be true that our ape ancestors ate meat, but it's also true that the meat they ate was mainly bugs. Most people I know do not find bugs appetizing, and we don't know what they would do for our health. Also, researchers believe that eating insects might be detrimental to the environment and our ecosystem. [11]

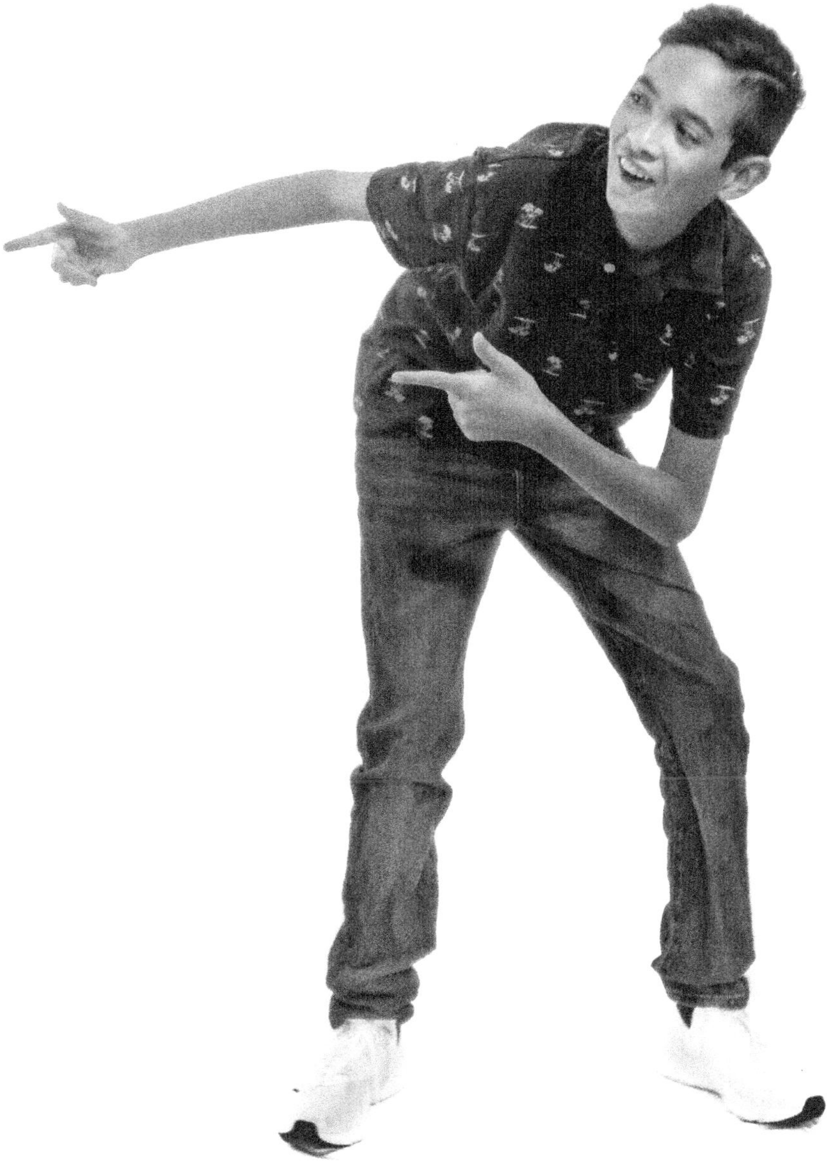

7

Attack:

I heard that (insert stupid diet here) also works for getting healthy!

Comeback:

Oh, so you're on that diet? Are you referring to actual research or something you read on social media?

Explanation:

Most of the diets that people will try to say are better than vegan aren't even half-decent. Many diets can give temporary results, but are you looking at the long-term results? The Paleo diet is popular. The idea is that our evolutionary ancestors were mainly eating meat. More recent research indicates that our early human ancestors, Australopithecus to Homosapiens in eastern Africa, were actually mainly vegan.[31] The ketogenic diet is currently popular as well, where people can eat unlimited meat and dairy, but no fruit and limited vegetables. This is dangerous long term, considering that the vitamins and minerals we need come from fruits and vegetables and there is evidence that meat and dairy cause diseases like cancer, autoimmune, and heart diseases. [2, 32,33,34,35,36]

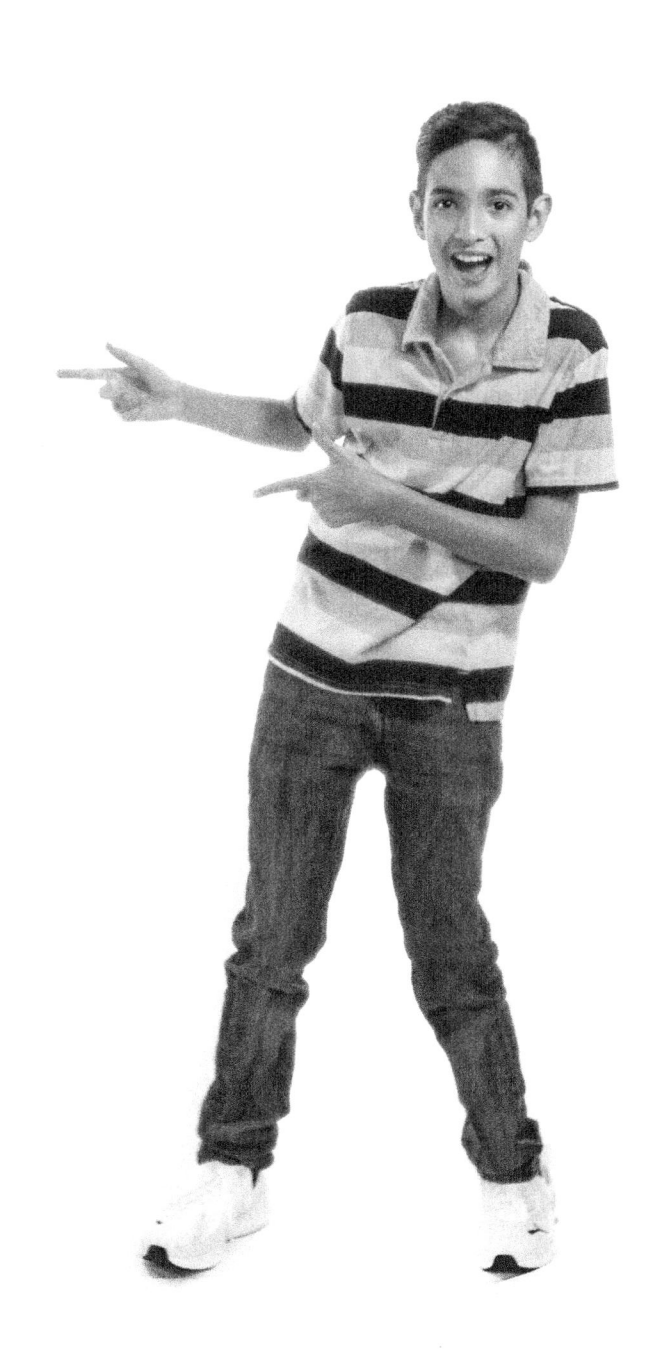

Attack:

But being vegan isn't healthy.

Comeback:

Says who? While eating vegan junk like fries or chips is unhealthy, healthy vegan diets have been shown to prevent and reverse deadly diseases like heart disease and autoimmune diseases. Meat and dairy cause heart disease and cancer! You need to check your sources!

Explanation:

There has been an explosion in books and documentaries proving the benefits of vegan diets. Healthy vegan diets have been shown to prevent and reverse deadly diseases like heart disease[32] and autoimmune diseases.[34, 35]. My mother was able to completely reverse her own Lupus over 15 years ago, and was able to have me after her doctors said she couldn't have children, all because of a healthy vegan diet.[34] On the other hand, research has shown that dairy causes cancer, obesity, autoimmune diseases, and heart disease.[33, 32, 34] Also, meat has been classified as a carcinogen by the World Health Organization based on the accumulation of scientific research from scientists all over the world.[2] If it's good health you're after, go vegan!

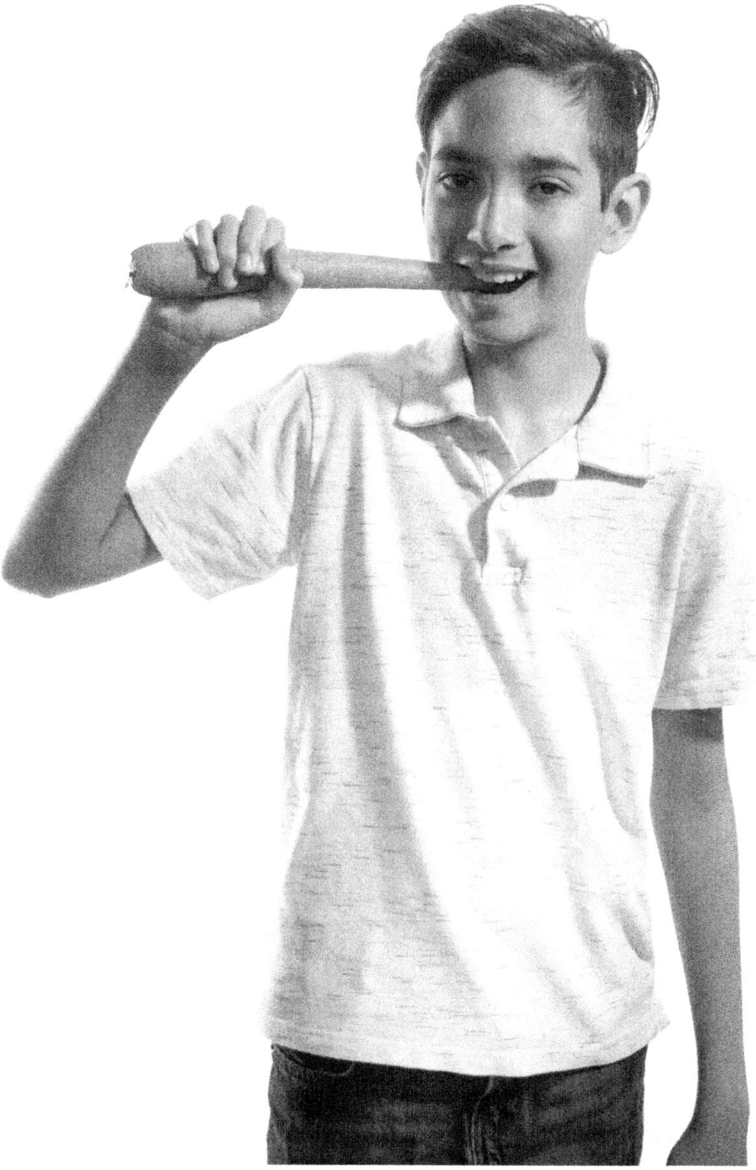

9

Attack:

The Big One: where do you get your protein?

Comeback:

Plants. (Too easy)

Explanation:

Most people think that meat is the best source of protein, but in reality, meat is the biggest source of heart attacks.[36] Amino acids are the building blocks of proteins, and are available in every plant we eat. Worried there isn't enough protein in plants? Let's consider the largest carnivores versus herbivores walking on the land. The largest carnivore on land is the polar bear who can weigh 1000 pounds (adult female) to 1700 pounds (adult male).[39] The largest herbivore is the African Elephant which can weigh 6,600 pounds (adult female) to 13,000 pounds (adult male)![37] Not only that, African elephants typically live twice as long as Polar Bears[39]. So, plants build bigger and healthier beasts!

31

10

Attack:

But meat gives you more protein so it's better.

Comeback:

More protein isn't a good thing. High protein diets have been shown to raise your risk of cancer and heart disease.

Explanation:

Most people think that if you get a lot of protein in, you're going to be really big and strong, but most people eat way more protein than they need, and overeating meat raises your risks of obesity, heart disease, and cancers.[12, 2, 32, 33] If you eat plants, you can get muscular without having to worry about harming your health.[40]

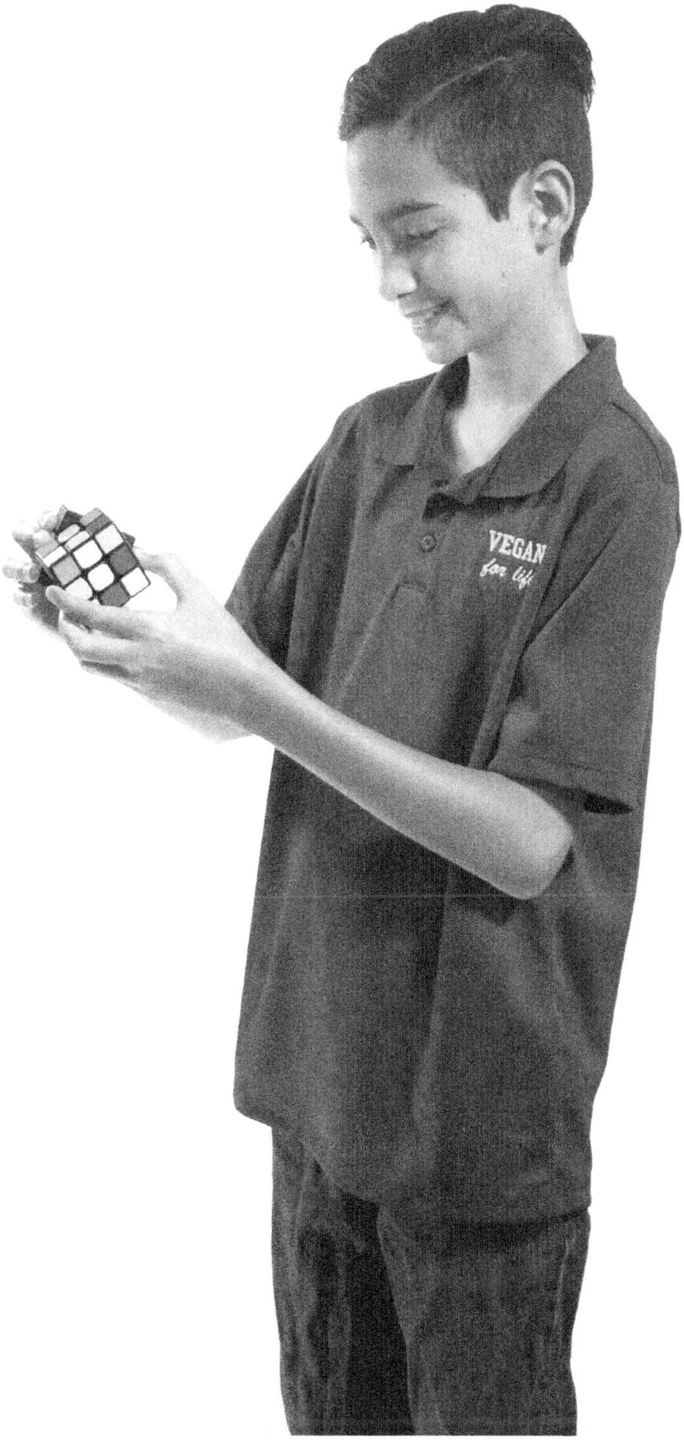
VEGAN

11

Attack:

You need meat to be strong.

Comeback:

Compare the biggest living land herbivore and carnivore, who is bigger? An elephant sure looks strong compared to that polar bear or lion! As for humans, eating meat is more likely to make you fat than make you strong.

Explanation:

Whenever somebody tries to pull this argument, I usually laugh in their face. I might personally be skinny, but it doesn't have anything to do with my diet, it's because I prefer running over lifting weights. According to research, meat is more likely to make you fat than make you strong.[30] What makes you strong isn't your diet, it's exercise. If you want to be strong, play sports or lift heavy weights at the gym. That is a sure way to get strong.[30]

Eating plants and lifting weights will make you strong! There have been bodybuilders winning competitions who are 100% vegan. Recently, A vegan athlete, Massimo Brunaccioni, became the Men's Physique World Champion WNBF at the Natural World Bodybuilding Championship.[42]

One of the world's strongest men, Patrik Baboumian, is vegan. He was the 2012 European Powerlifting Champion and a world record breaker in three strongman events.[41] In fact, my father proved that people can build twice as much muscle in less time with half the protein intake of meat-eating bodybuilders.[40]

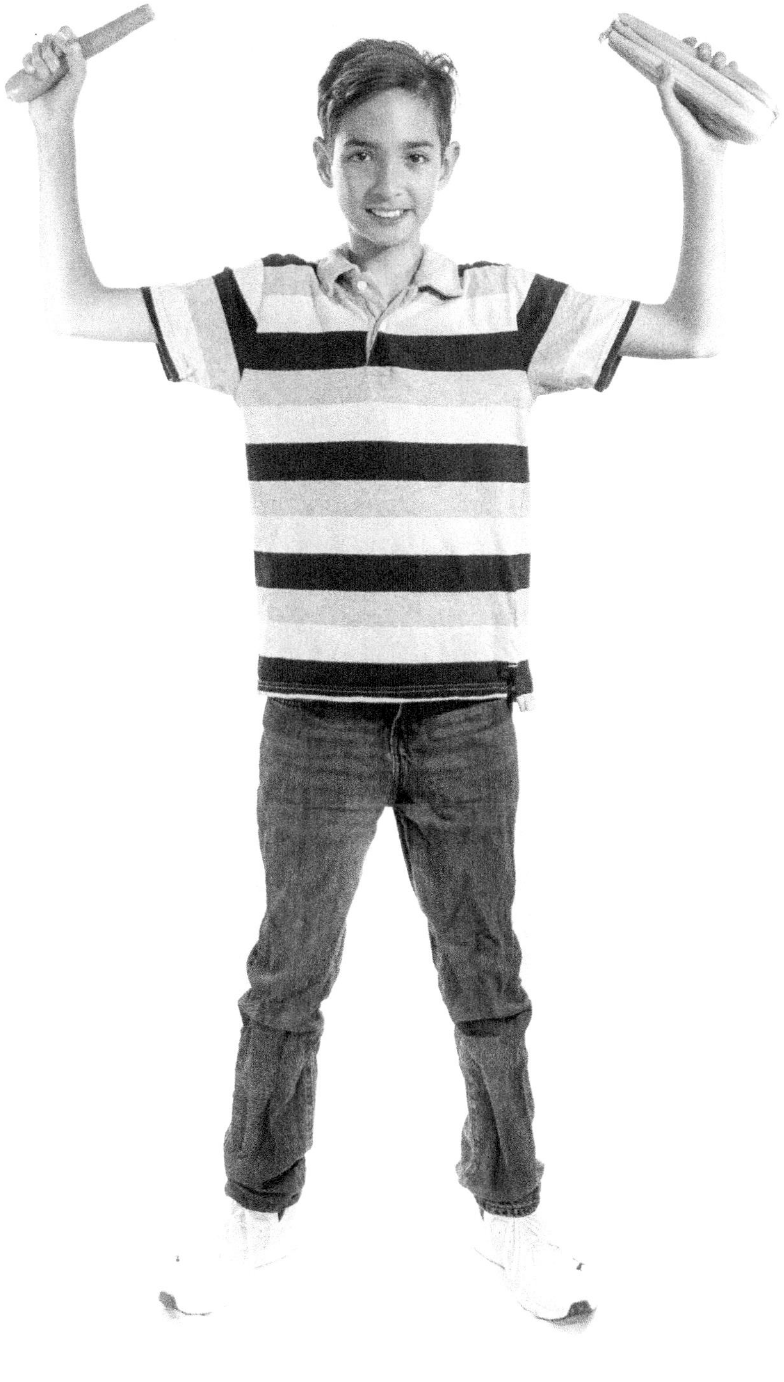

12

Attack:

Milk gives calcium and you don't drink milk, so you are calcium deficient.

Comeback:

Actually, studies have shown that people who drink milk are more likely to have bone fractures. You want calcium? Eat broccoli.

Explanation:

It's true, milk does the inverse of helping our bones. When it was studied, they found high dairy intake was associated with more bone fractures, not less![43] Dairy has also been shown to cause cancer.[33] Milk is one of those things where when you weigh the pros and cons, there really aren't any pros. I think most people just drink milk because of addiction or they are misinformed. It's most likely both. It's the same deal with cheese. Cheese is just compressed and solid milk, so it's got a higher dose of the unhealthy stuff.[13]

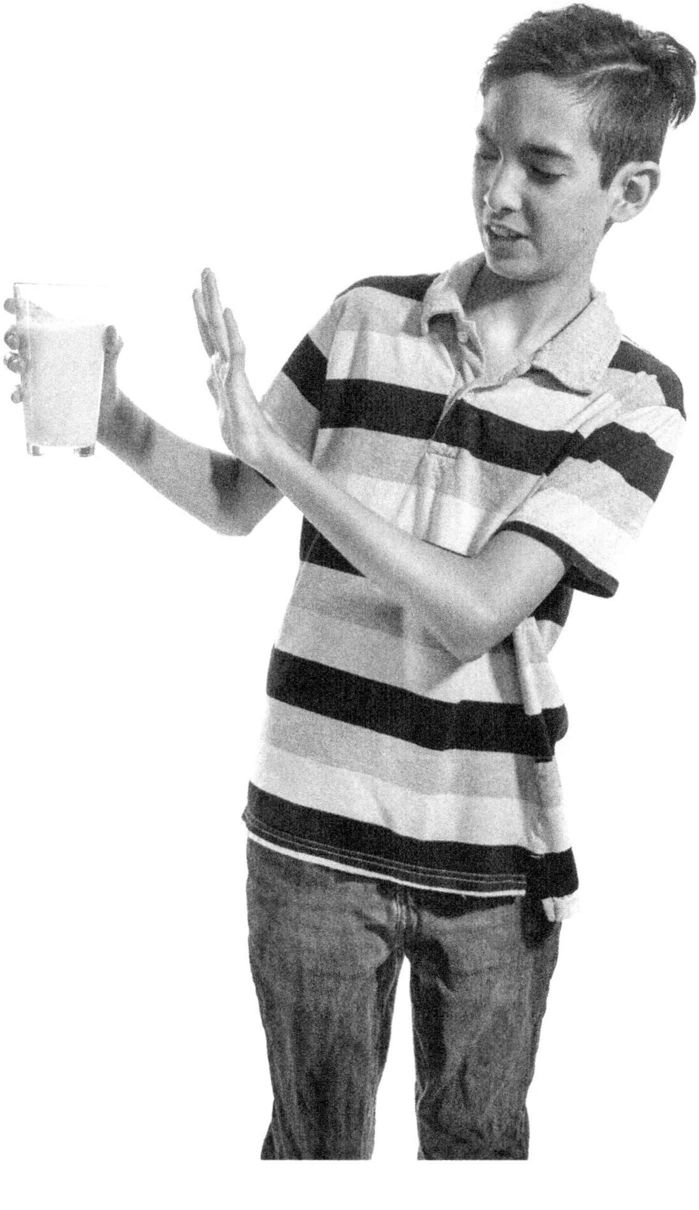

13

Attack:

I only eat range-free chickens and eggs.

Comeback:

Aww that's cute, they can run free before they meet their untimely deaths.

Explanation:

We are led to believe that free-range means that before the chickens are killed they get to run free in a contained area. However, the truth is that their lives are still miserable. While the hens might not be kept in cages, most still have their beaks cut off and are stuffed into dirty dark buildings where they never get to run free or even go outside at all. Male chicks on egg farms are killed on the spot either by being ground up or left out in garbage bags because they don't lay eggs.[24]

Free-range is definitely better than the factory farms which cramp the chickens in tiny cages for their whole lives, but in the end, taking chickens' freedom and their eggs and then later killing them is cruel no matter how much space they have.

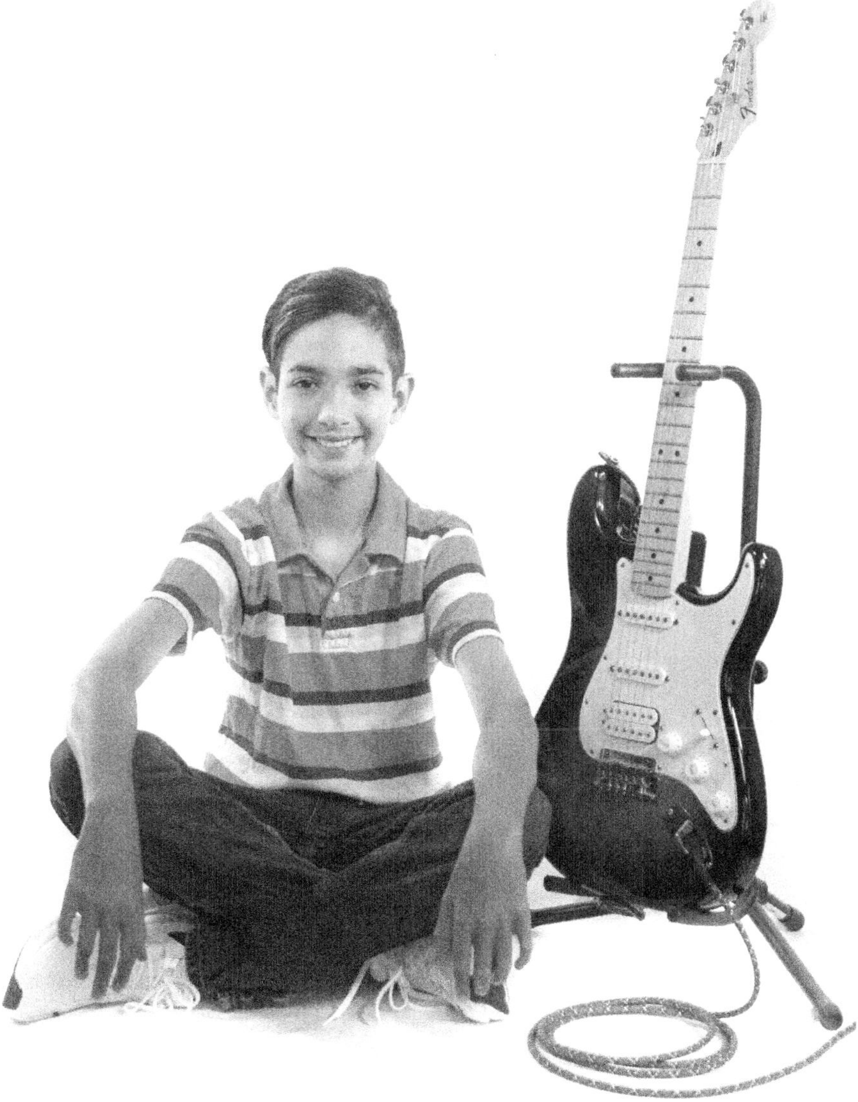

14

Attack:

Ok if meat is bad, I'll be vegetarian.

Comeback:

I am glad you want to help animals. But if you really want to help them, being vegetarian is not enough. For cows to make milk, they must make babies, and those babies are killed for veal so we can drink their milk. Chickens suffer so much when we take their eggs. It's still cruel.

Explanation:

I am glad you want to save animals and eat healthier! Vegetarianism is a really good start, but it isn't the best.[45] If you're a vegetarian, just take the next step. You can remove one food at a time if you would like. I know a few people who are doing that and succeeding. The only issue with vegetarianism is that you still have eggs, milk, and cheese.[18,13] Just take the next step. I know you can do it!

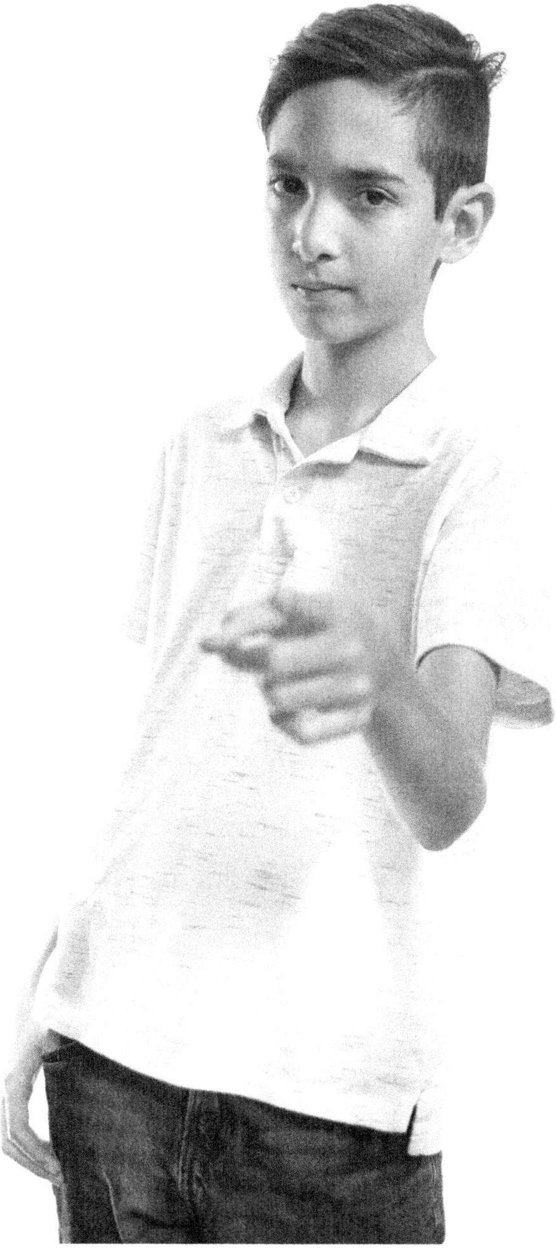

15

Attack:

But if we didn't eat them, animals would take over.

Comeback:

If we stop eating meat, people will stop breeding animals and that scenario will never happen.

Explanation:

Think about it. Humans are currently breeding animals to be killed. What happens if they no longer kill? They stop breeding. It's pretty simple. There is no need to worry about overpopulation because nature would return to normal. Animals never overpopulated before humans started breeding them, so who says they would afterward? It's just science. Besides, the only species currently overpopulating the planet are humans! [44]

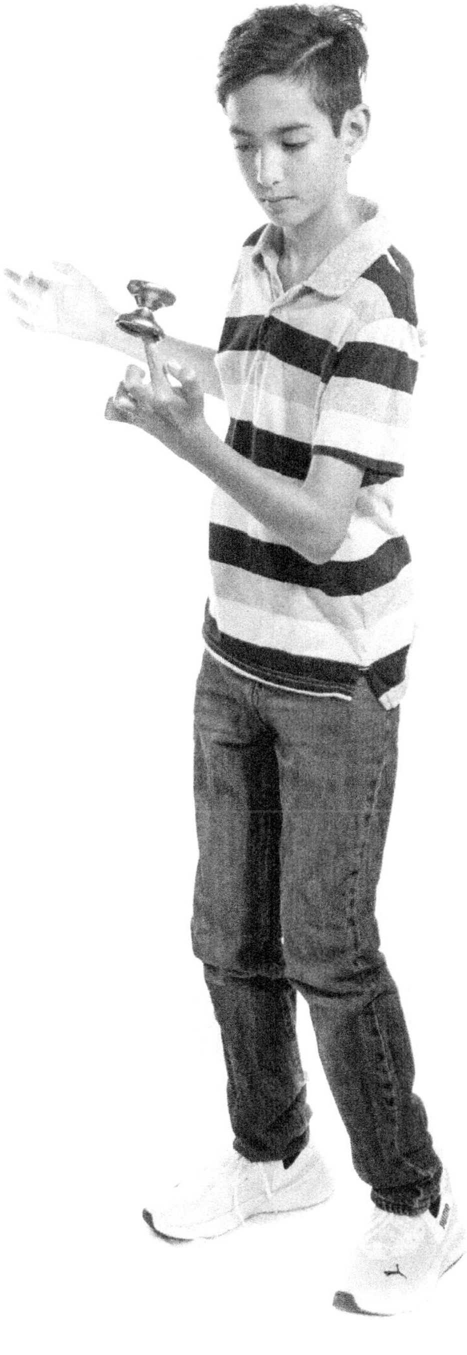

16

Attack:

What about if I'm somewhere cold during the winter, where no plants can grow?

Comeback:

Ever hear of a supermarket?

Explanation:

I am not sure which is more surprising, the fact that someone would actually bring up this argument or how easy of an explanation this is. First of all, why are you thinking of bizarre scenarios where suddenly you are in a frozen wasteland with no food? It makes no sense. Most of us buy our food in supermarkets, where they import food from places where it has the perfect conditions for growing fruits and vegetables.

45

Attack:

But I could never give up bacon.

Comeback:

Bacon isn't worth your life.

Explanation:

Bacon causes colon cancer and could make you lose parts of your colon or even your life.[2] Bacon is similar to smoking. It is addictive but has some terrible long-term effects. In fact, bacon and other processed meats like bologna and hot dogs have been classified in the same category of carcinogens as asbestos and smoking by the World Health Organization![2] I believe in you. You can do it.

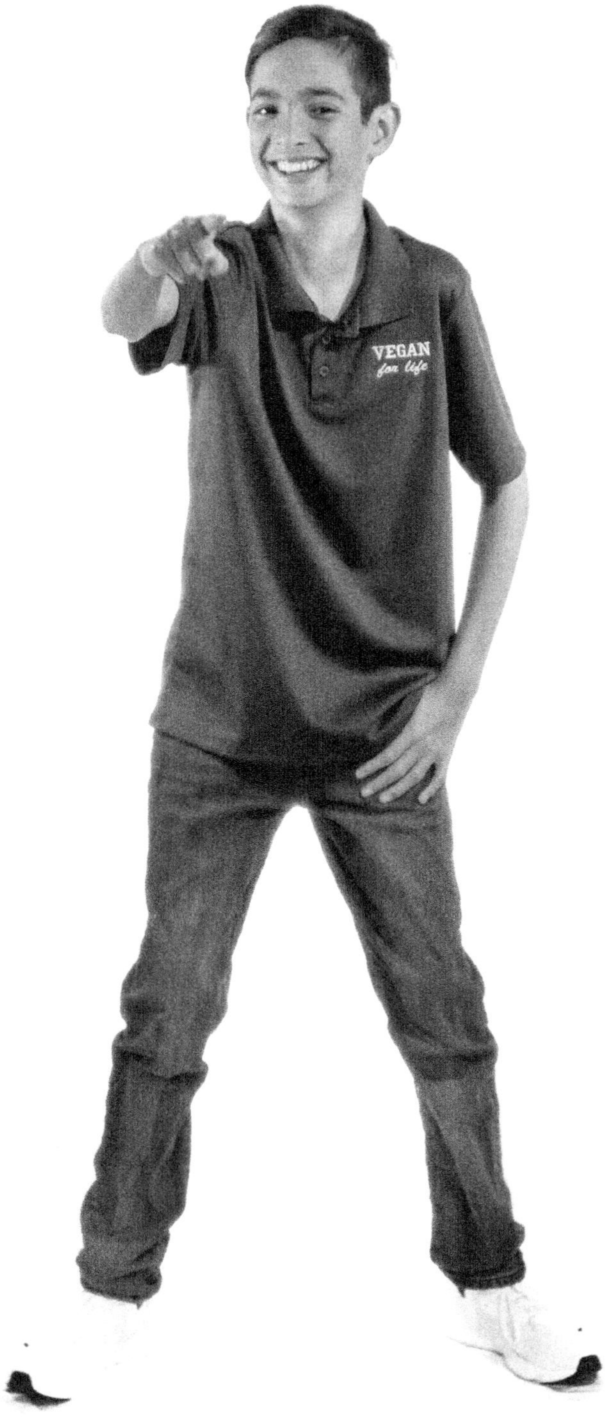
VEGAN
for life

Attack:

But vegetables are gross.

Comeback:

So, you don't like French fries?

Explanation:

I hear this argument a lot. People always try to tell me that my food is gross and vegetables taste terrible. It is not true. The average vegan enjoys most of the same food that most of the Earth eats, without any meat and dairy products, like veggie burgers, beans, grains, and yes, fruits and vegetables. In the end, I think we can all agree that everyone likes French fries.

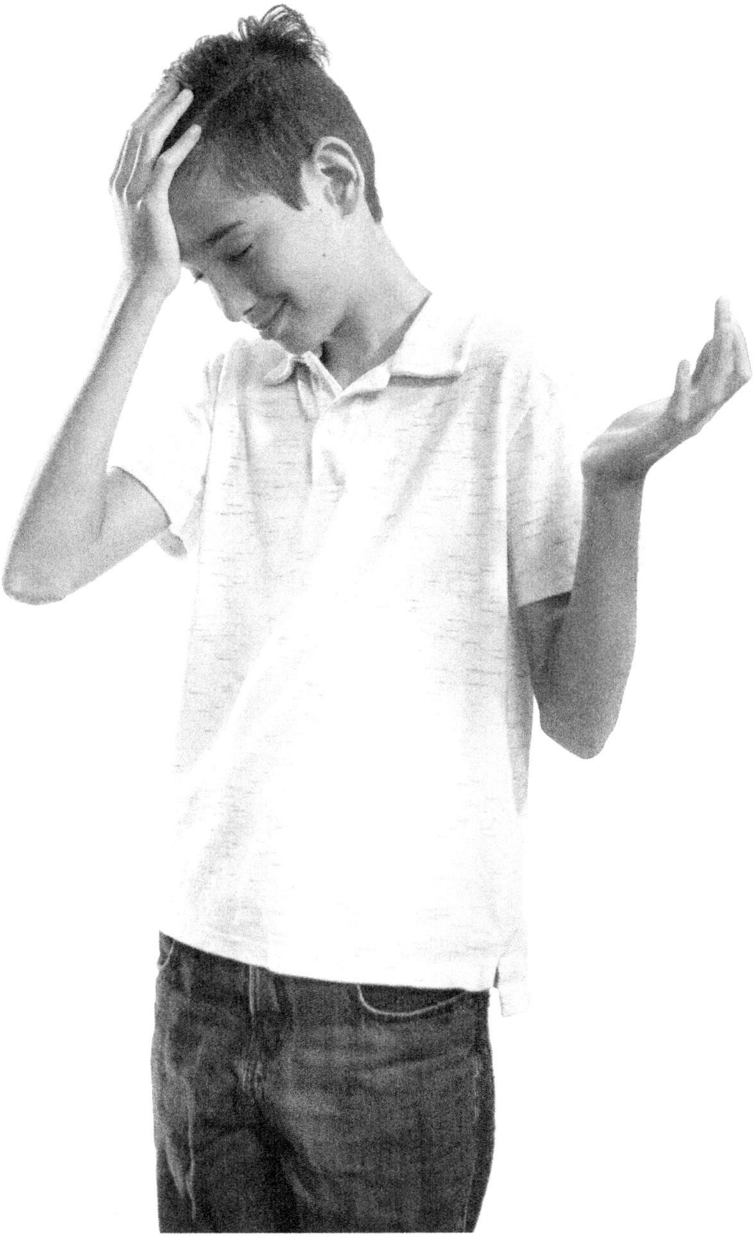

19

Attack:

You care more about animal suffering than human suffering.

Comeback:

You don't have to choose between animals and people.

Explanation:

Both animal suffering and human suffering are big deals. One of them is a little less heard of. Animals can't speak up for themselves, and while abusing cats and dogs is illegal in the USA, abusing and killing farm animals is not a crime. You never see PIG KILLED BY FARMER all over the news. So, farm animals need humans to speak up for them. Human suffering is bad, and we should do all we can to help humans in need; and other beings' suffering is just as bad if not worse and they need us too.

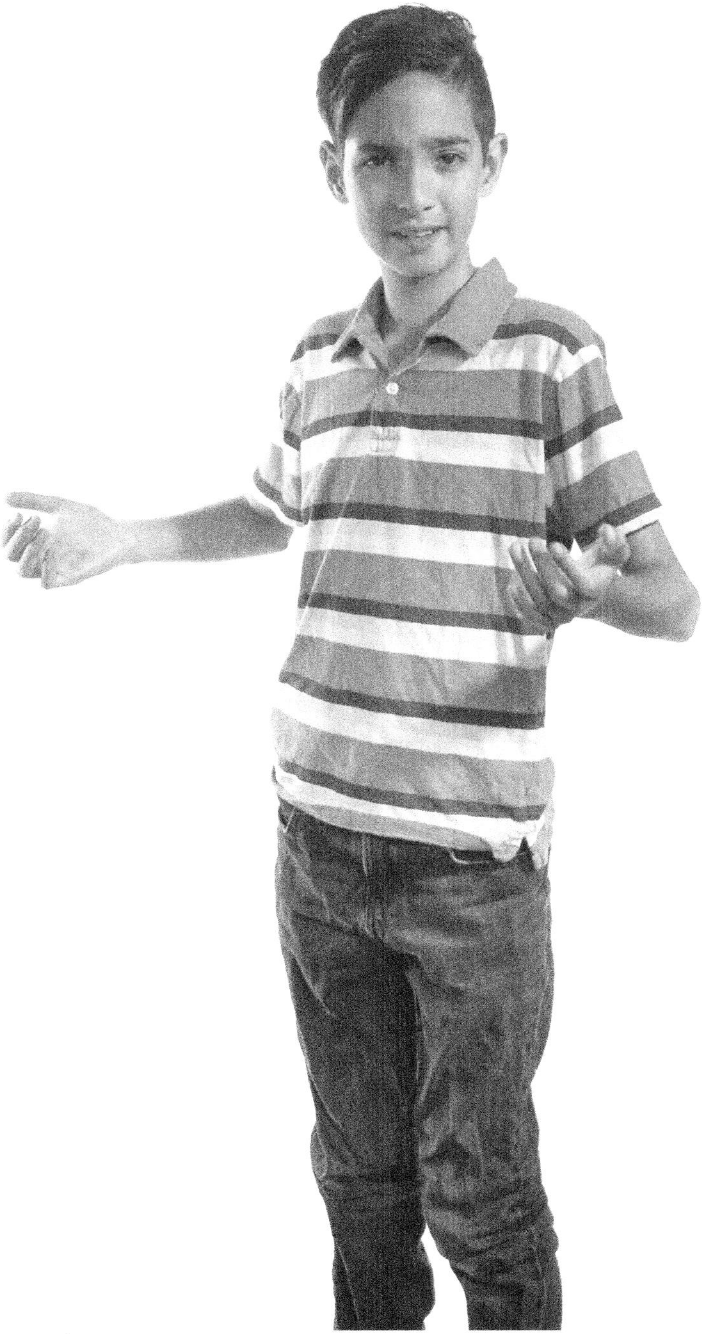

20

Attack:

Just one person won't make a difference.

Comeback:

Who knows, someone you turn vegan may be the next president and make the whole country vegan.

Explanation:

Saying that one person won't make a difference is a terrible excuse. You have no idea who you will grow up to be. You could end up being a celebrity animal rights activist and convert thousands of people to veganism. Even if you are the only person who becomes vegan, you will save thousands of animal lives. Did you know that over twenty-six animals a year are killed per person who eats meat? That stacks up to one thousand eight hundred twenty animals per lifetime.[14]

When you think about that, going vegan means you will save thousands of animals with a dietary choice. That means your choice makes a difference to those animals.[14]

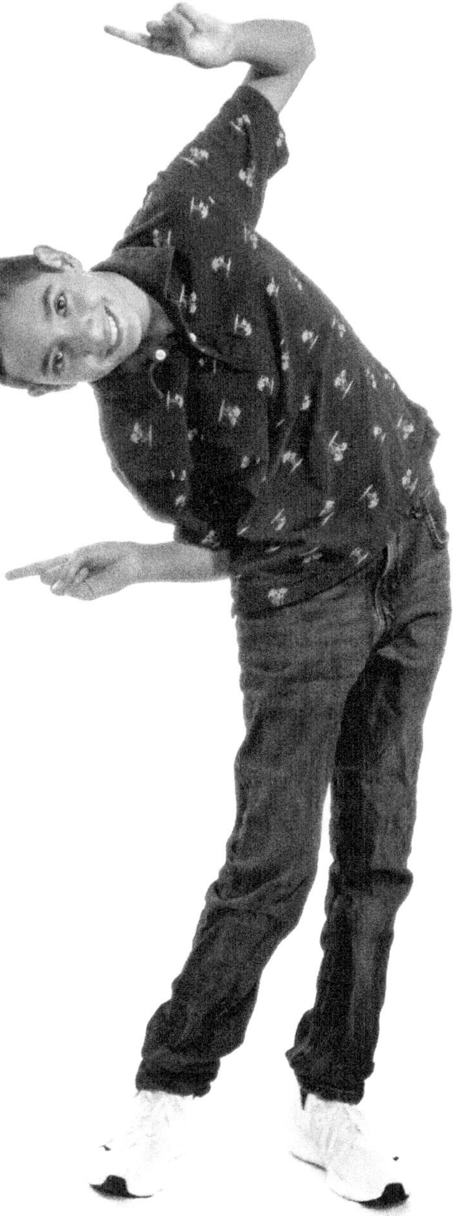

21

Attack:

I throw fish back when I go fishing.

Comeback:

Ok, you shove a steel hook down their throats and pull them up by stabbing it through their cheeks, then throw them back to die from shock? Very kind of you.

Explanation:

Imagine you are a fish. You see a little bit of food dangling from a string of some sort. You are a little suspicious, but free food is still free food. You decide to bite your prey, only to have a hook pierce through your cheek and yank you upwards out of the water where you can't breath. Somebody picks you up and tears the hook out of your cheek and throws you back in the water. You are in pain, and then suffocating, and then thrown back still bleeding and in pain. Many fish don't actually survive after being pulled out of the water this way and die of shock. Even if they survive, fishing and then throwing fish back is still cruel.[15]

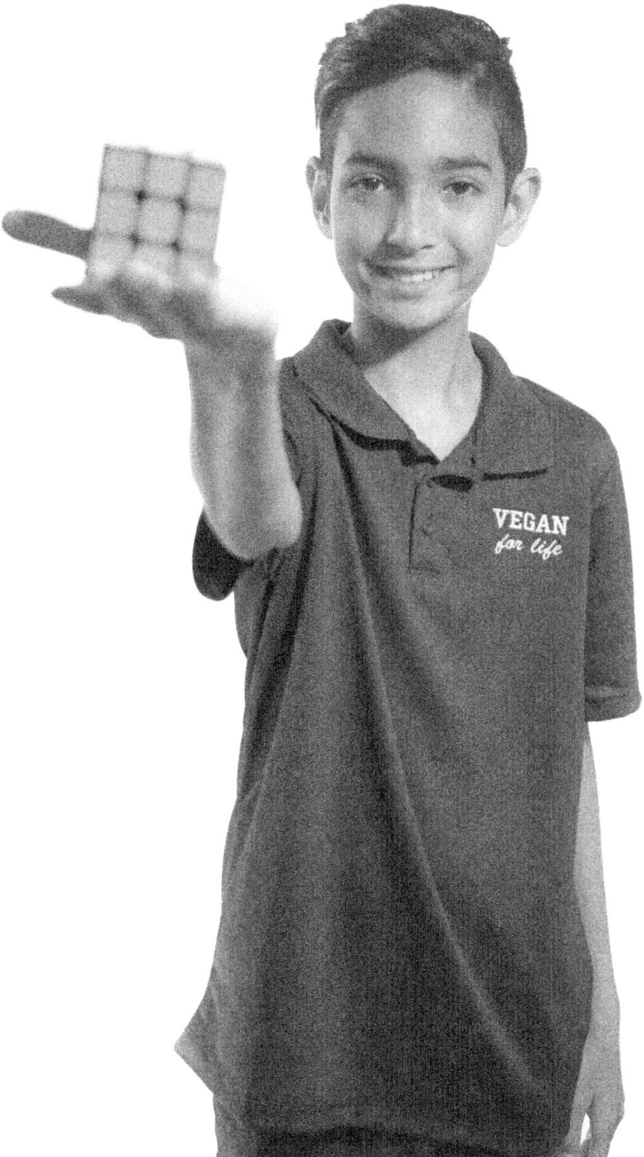
VEGAN
for life

Attack:

But humans are superior.

Comeback:

That gives us the responsibility to help those who are weaker, not kill them.

Explanation:

Superiority is not control, it is responsibility. Humans have taken over due to a knack for invention. Humans being superior has nothing to do with dietary choices though. People use this as an excuse quite a bit, but I believe that the more power we have, the more responsibility we have to wield it with compassion and care for those who are weaker than us. However, remember, superiority is not invincibility. Even if humans are superior, they will still get sick and die from eating meat and dairy products. I guess that's justice or karma in a way.

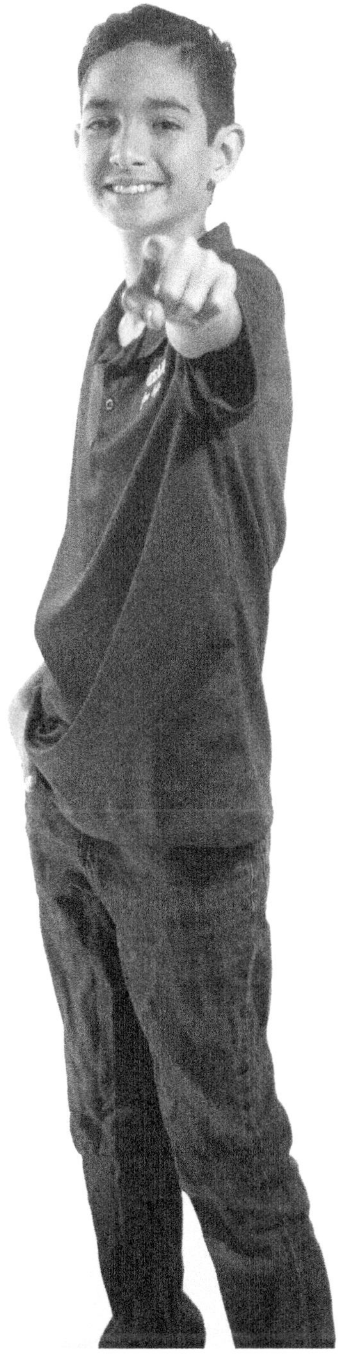

23

Attack:

But humans are smarter, don't we deserve control.

Comeback:

Unfortunately, not all humans are smarter (gesture toward whoever you're speaking to).

(I try to educate rather than insult, but some comments are just too ridiculous to respond in any other way.)

Explanation:

Being smarter has nothing to do with control. Even if we had control, that doesn't give us the right to harm or murder without reason. In fact, humans might not be as smart as you think. Dogs are able to respond to commands in our language, but we still haven't figured out how to speak dog.

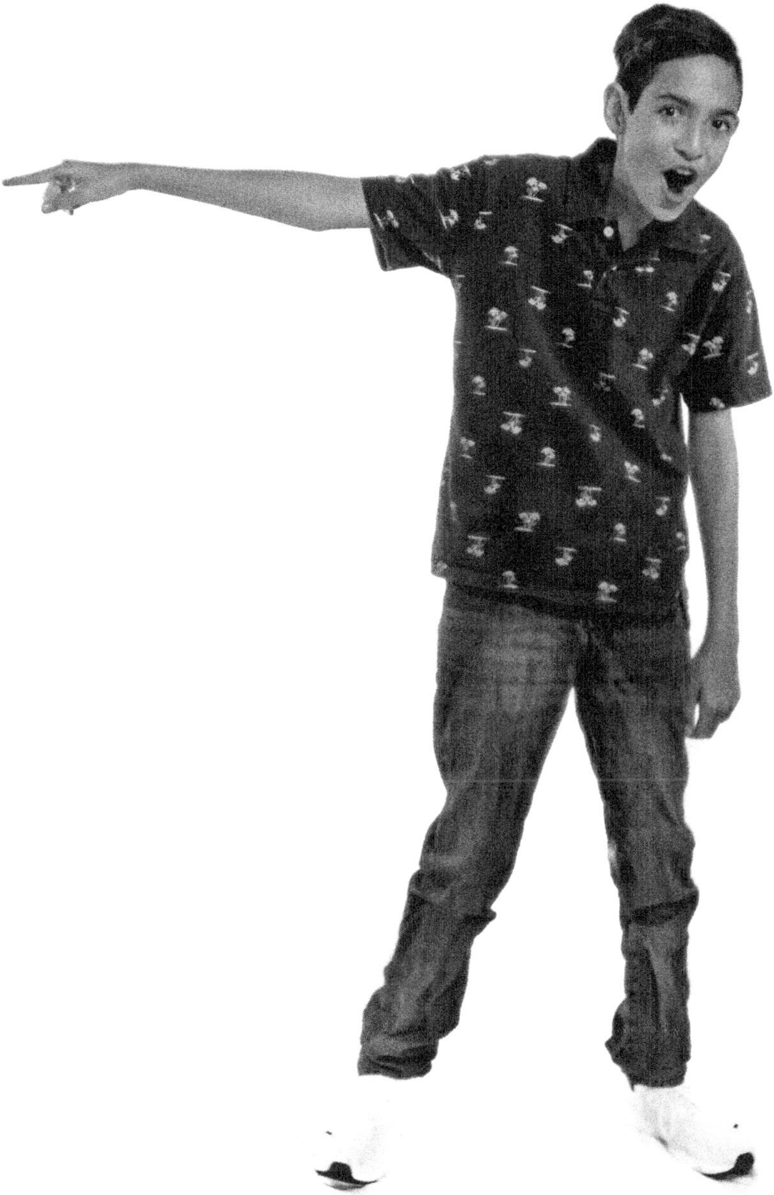

24

Attack:

But humans are carnivores.

Comeback:

Ha Ha. So, you hunt and kill animals with your bare hands and teeth and eat the entire animal from head to toe, raw and bleeding? I'd like to see that!

Explanation:

Humans are not carnivores. Humans are not omnivores. Humans are herbivores. Think about it: a carnivore has the ability to capture and kill another animal without any tools besides its teeth and claws. Then it eats the entire animal raw and bleeding, including the veins, the brains, the organs, the skin, and the muscles. If you were a carnivore, what I just wrote would actually make you hungry. If you found it gross, it means you are not a carnivore!

Humans can get deadly infections from eating raw meat or blood. Carnivores do not get sick from eating dead animals. Humans are built to eat plants. We can pluck a fruit or vegetable from a plant and eat it right up and just absorb all the vitamins and minerals. Yum! The reason we have color vision is so we can identify ripe fruits and vegetables. Carnivore eyes are trained to sense the movement of their prey and don't need to see color. Our teeth are flat and move side to side to chew up plant matter, just like other herbivores, not up and down like a carnivore.[16, 28, 46]

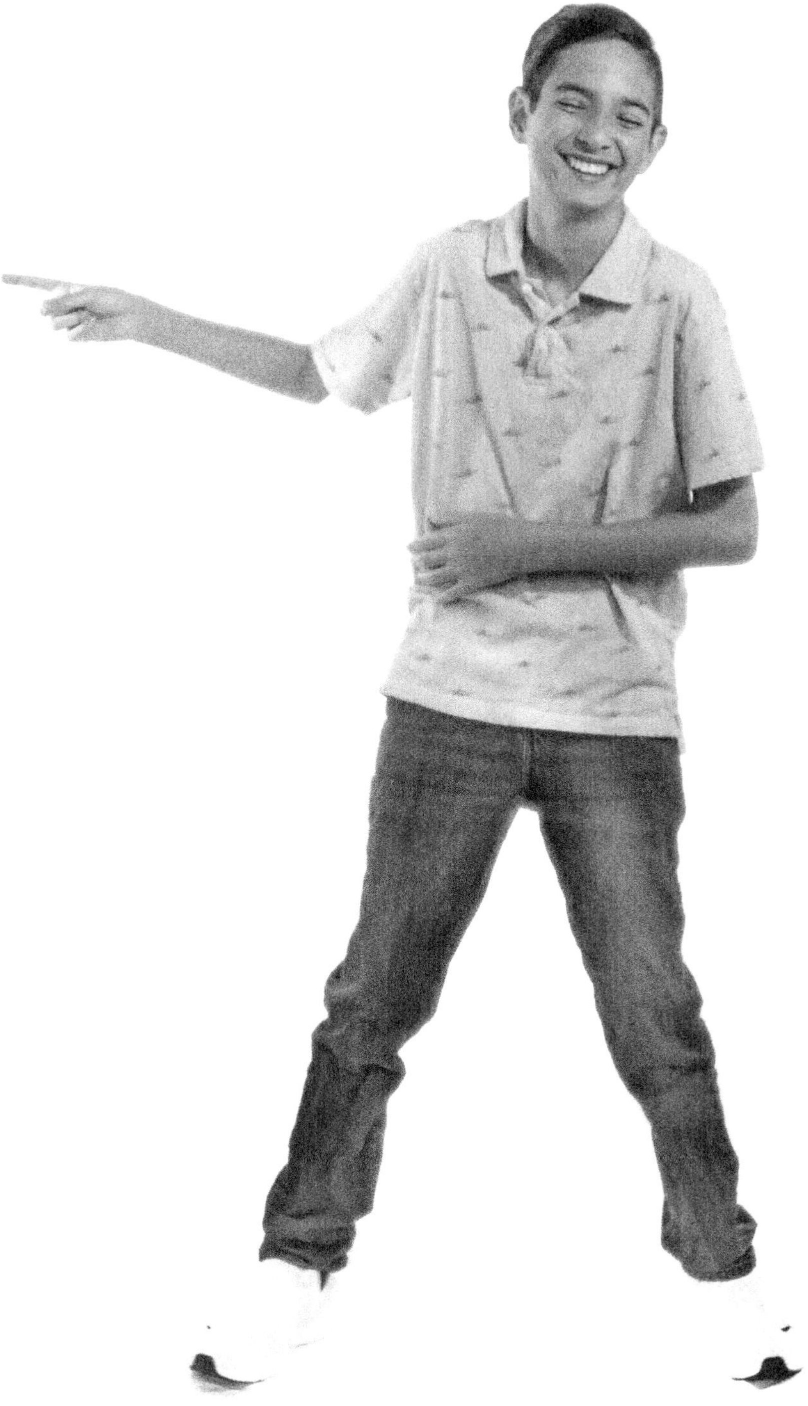

25

Attack:

How come you're skinny (only answer if you're skinny).

Comeback:

Because I'm healthy, but I can't say the same for you.

Explanation:

If people are making fun of you because you're skinny, then that means that they have nothing else they can find in you that makes you imperfect. Skinny isn't even an imperfection though. When you're an adult, skinny is a compliment and many people have to put in hours at the gym to get there, so that just means you have nothing else to make fun of.

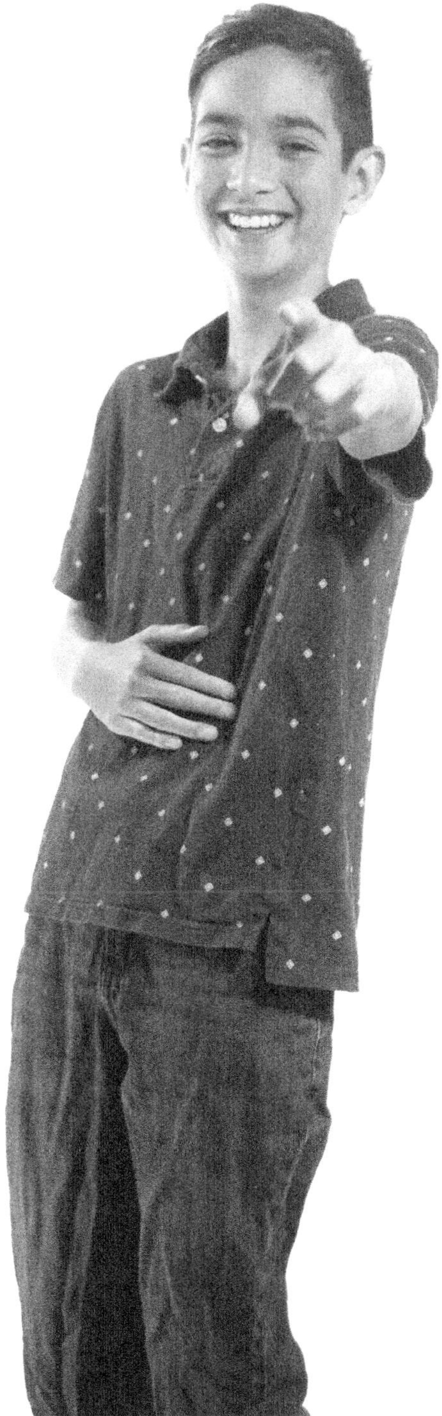

26

Attack:

God put animals here to eat.

Comeback:

Why would God give them pain receptors then?

Explanation:

If animals were purely meant for eating, then they wouldn't have emotions and pain receptors. No emotions or pain receptors? That sounds familiar! Oh right, plants have neither of those. Plants literally grow fruit, and the only purpose of the fruit is to be eaten. That is how plants reproduce. When animals eat the fruit, they poop the seeds.[17] Besides, for your friends who want to quote the bible as evidence about diet, tell them to read Genesis 1:29 where it says that God made the plants and trees for us to eat.[47]

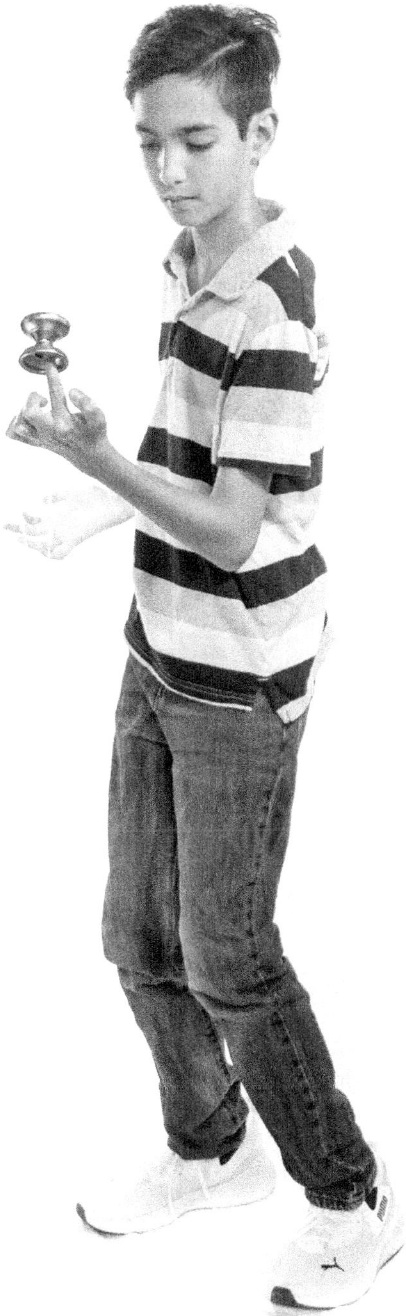

Attack:

But the dairy industry doesn't kill cows.

Comeback:

Actually they do. Just like people, cows need to get pregnant to produce milk. So farmers force them to get pregnant, then they kill the baby calves to steal their milk for people.

Explanation:

The dairy industry is very cruel. Farmers keep milk production high by continuously impregnating female cows. Because they want to make as much money as possible from selling milk, the farmer takes the baby cows away immediately. Female calves are raised to make more dairy; they raise them in captivity until they can grow up to be another milk cow, hooked up to a machine their whole lives.[18]

The males calves are put in tiny crates where they cannot even turn around and are sold as veal. They are lonely and hungry and killed as babies because people like the soft meat of veal.

Mother cows want to raise their babies and they cry for weeks when their babies are taken from them. Instead of cuddling and feeding their baby, they forever pump milk into a painful machine against their own will.[18]

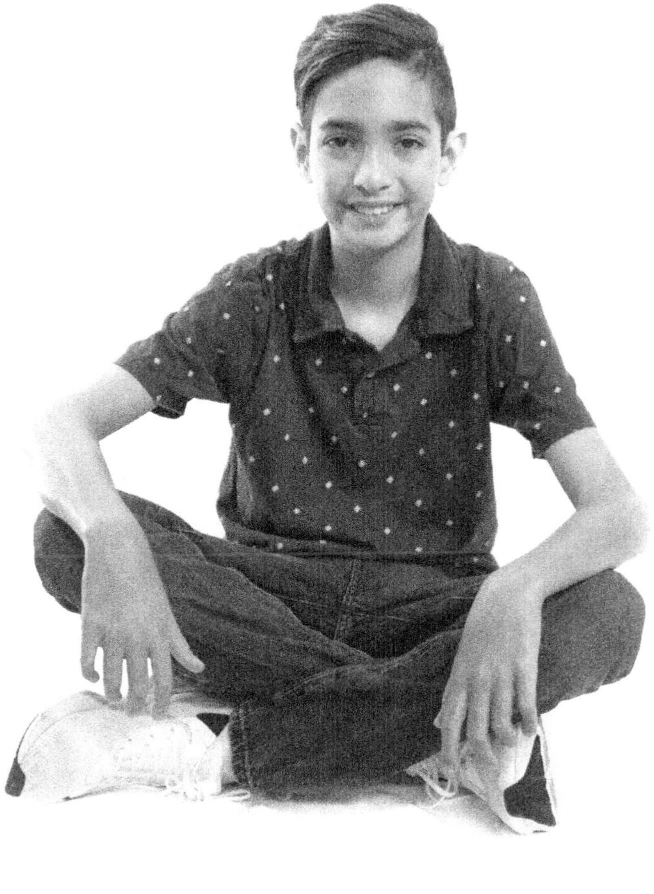

Attack:

But people will lose their jobs if we stop eating meat.

Comeback:

So, should we do the wrong thing to save jobs? Maybe we should stick with coal and oil rather than renewable energy too? Humans have to evolve and we will find new jobs to replace obsolete ones.

Explanation:

If the meat and dairy industries collapse, people will lose their jobs and that's sad and all, but isn't killing millions of living beings much more important? Beyond the ethical issues, it turns out the meat and dairy industries are bad for the economy.[19] According to the National Academy of the Sciences, U.S. farms cost the economy more in health and environmental damage than they contribute to the economy.[19] Then add in the medical costs of all the diseases caused by eating animal products and it's even worse. Also, it won't happen overnight. As the meat industry starts to lose its funding, people will look for new jobs.[19] When meat and dairy farms are no longer profitable, the farmers can switch to growing plant foods instead and there will be more jobs available on the new farms.

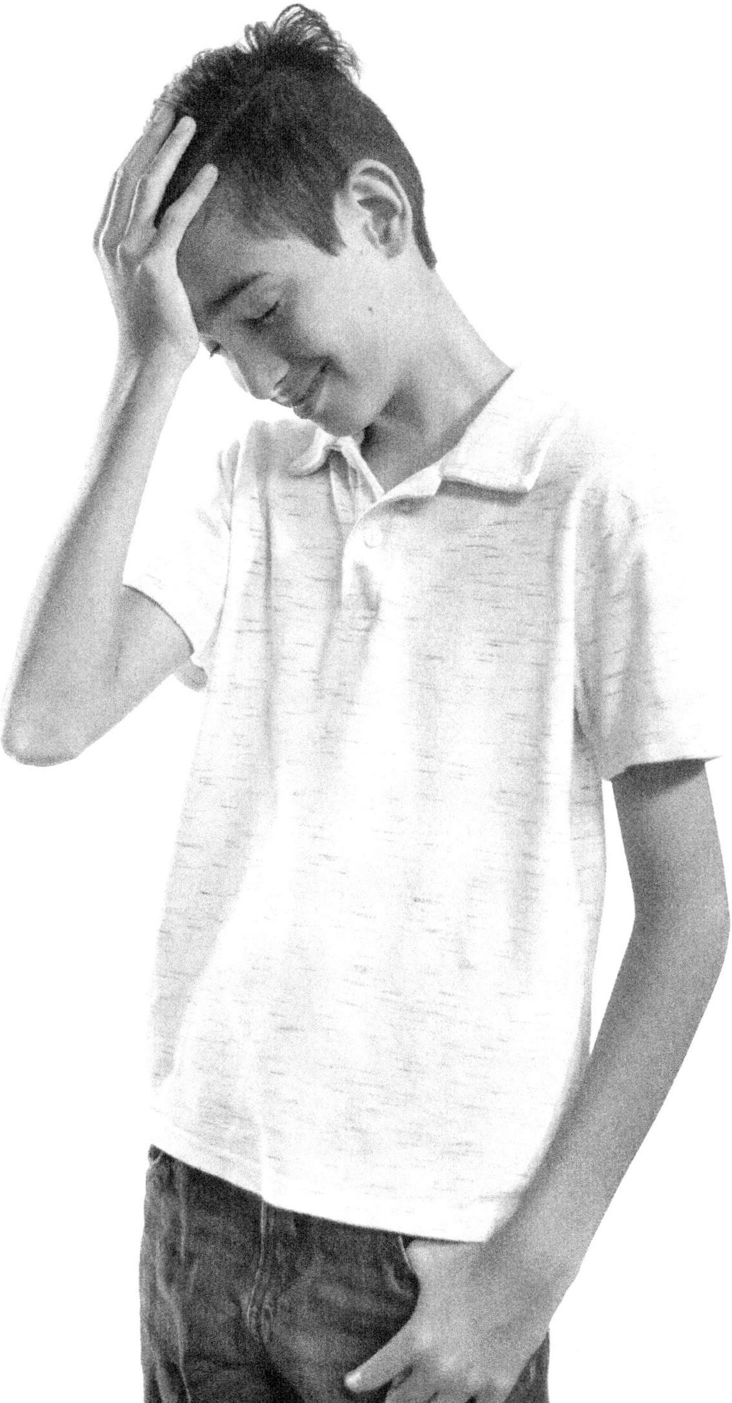

29

Attack:

Eating animals is completely legal, so it's obviously not wrong.

Comeback:

Slavery was once legal too. Just because something is legal, doesn't mean it's right.

Explanation:

Just because something is allowed doesn't mean it's the right thing to do. There have been many unethical things that weren't illegal. As I said, slavery was one of those. Segregation and discrimination of people in the USA was once legal even though it was wrong. Our country is still fighting for equal rights and protection for every human. Farm animals don't have legal protection under the law, so they need us to help them. Currently, eating and murdering animals is legal, but it's not right. Do the right thing even when the wrong thing is allowed, so you can be part of the positive change in this world!

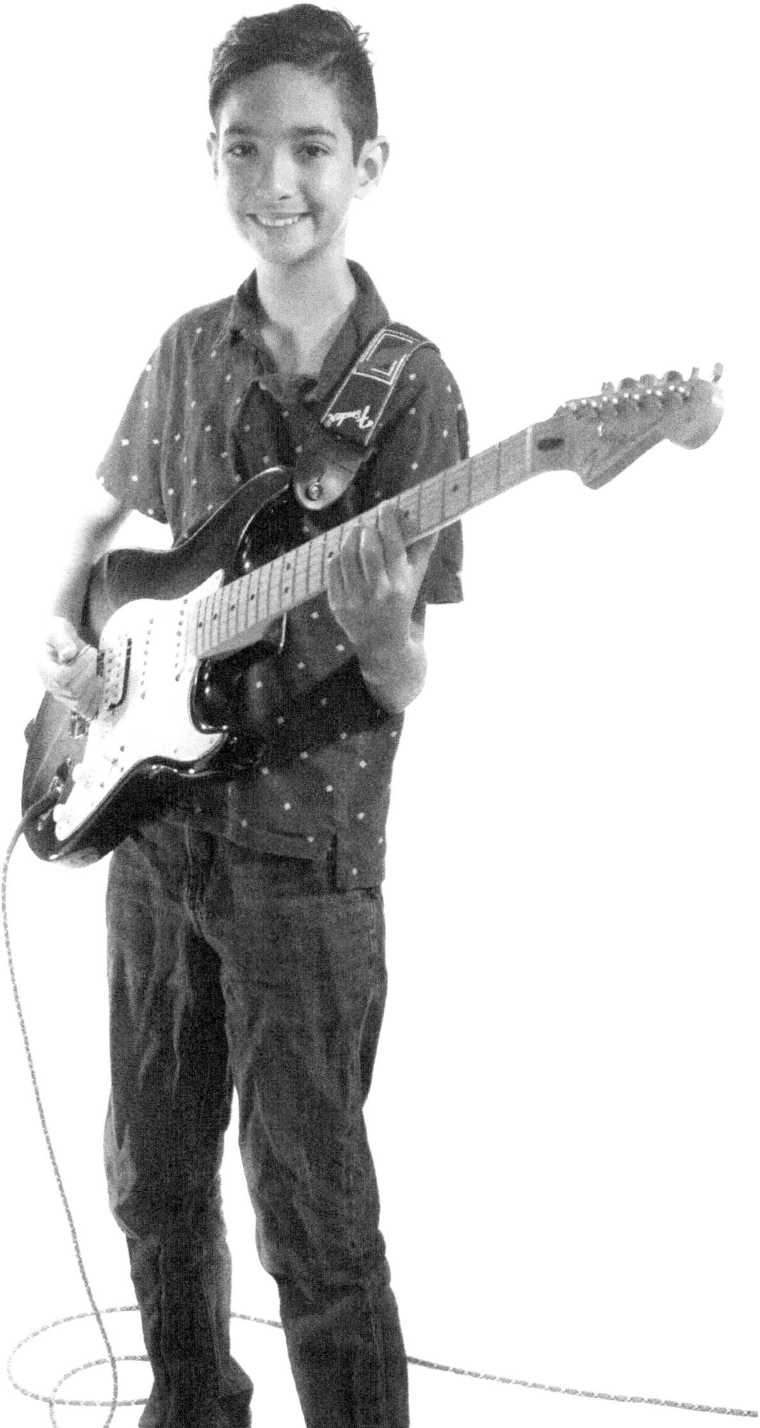

30

Attack:

But we can kill animals without pain, it's quick so they won't suffer.

Comeback:

First of all, murder is wrong whether it's painful or not, but second, they actually do not try to make the deaths painless or quick. The meat industry only cares about money, not how the animals feel.

Explanation:

The meat industry does not care if the animal hurts or not. It doesn't benefit the meat industry to kill animals without pain. They only kill for money, so they don't care a single bit if they are being ethical or not. Cows are forced to stand in line listening to the screams of other cows ahead of them as they fight to get free and witness the deaths of others in front of them. It is brutal and they are often still conscious and aware as they are being slaughtered. I don't want to put the details in a kids' book but your parents might be able to fill you in on the details, it's terrible. Even if it was somehow painless, I know murder is wrong, so even if they did kill without pain, I would still be vegan and against animal products. Every animal has the right to live and roam freely. Human rights is an important issue, but so are animal rights.

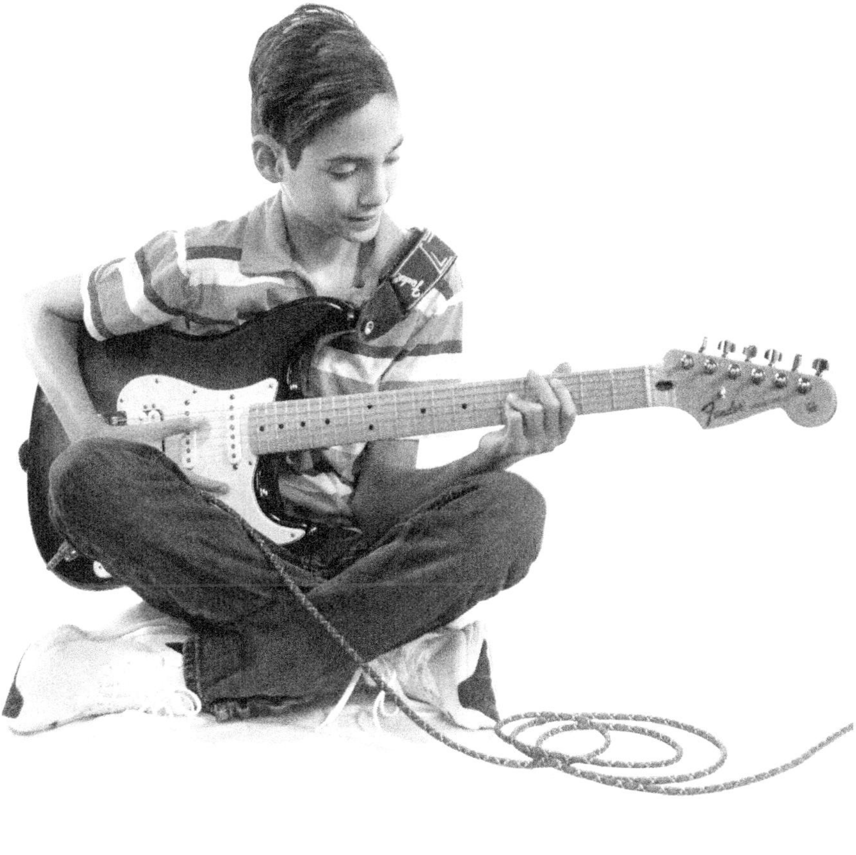

31

Attack:

What I eat is a personal choice.

Comeback:

Personal choice means it's only about you. This choice is about millions of lives and the fate of our planet.

Explanation:

I would rather do something that helps millions of people, animals, and the planet, rather than just myself. Saying that it's a personal choice is selfish and it isn't even a real answer. When people use this excuse, it just means that they ran out of excuses and are trying to leave the conversation without admitting they're wrong. If someone says this, that means that they are closing themselves off from any reasonability.

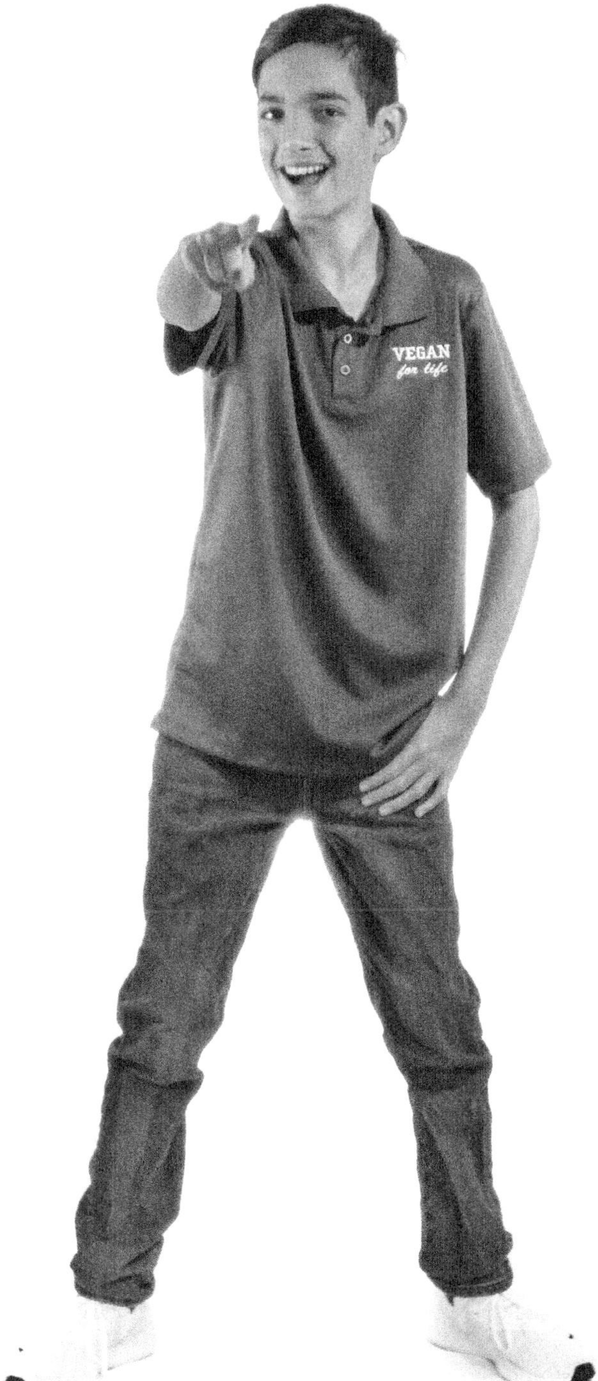
VEGAN
for life

32

Attack:

Vegans are so judgmental.

Comeback:

In order to say that, you must be judging vegans yourself. Stop being so judgmental.

Explanation:

People always try to call others judgmental or judgy, but by doing that, you are judging them, and therefore are a hypocrite. By the way, if someone is judging you, it has nothing to do with them being vegan. That just means that they are judgmental people. People are still people. Meat eaters are also judgmental. Saying that we are judgmental is pointless. What matters is that we are trying to do the right thing and save lives. I know we are saying things people don't want to hear, but that doesn't make it less right.

77

Attack:

How about you focus on more important issues.

Comeback:

What is more important than saving lives? Anyway, I can eat vegan food and focus on other important issues, tell me about some issues you care about.

Explanation:

I hear this a lot, and people just don't understand that it doesn't take effort and focus to be vegan. Vegans can focus on other issues while eating well. It may take some time to figure out your favorite recipes, but really you only need one new breakfast, lunch, and dinner and expand from there. The better we eat, the better we can focus! I have found that most vegans I have met are busy active people who have many areas of interest and advocacy. We can focus on many important issues while eating ethically and healthily.

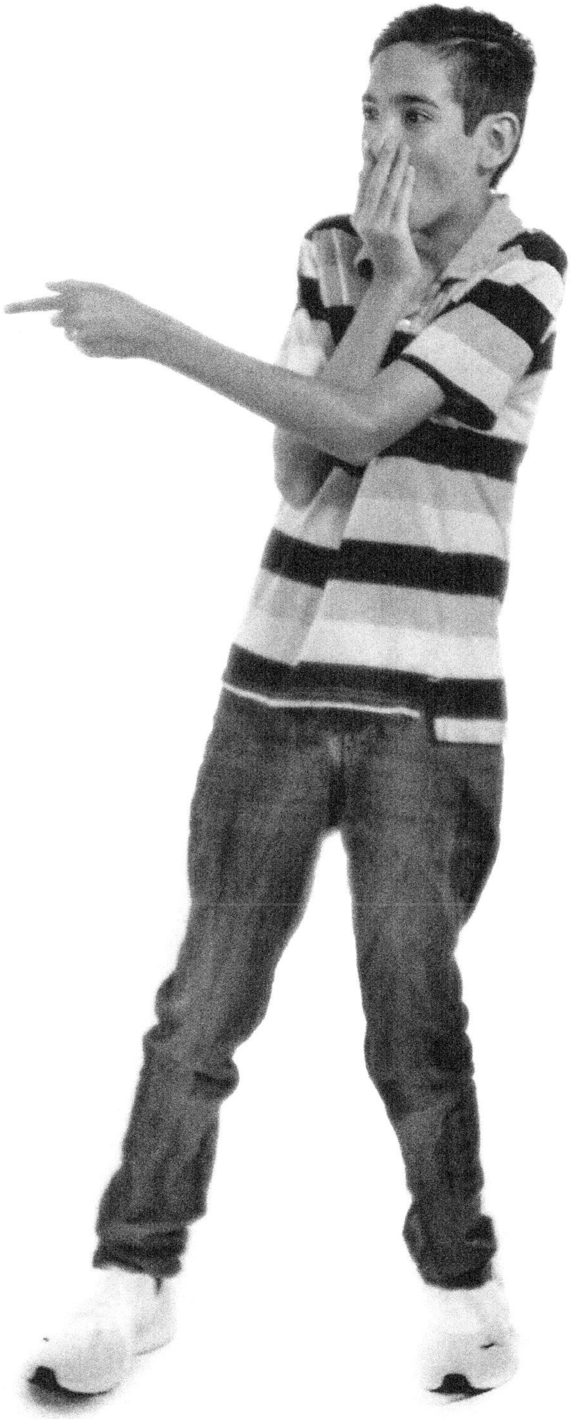

34

Attack:

Medication you take is tested on animals.

Comeback:

Veganism causes me to need less medication.

Explanation:

Sadly, medicine is tested on animals, but sometimes, you just don't have any other options. The good thing is, vegans are much less likely to get sick, so I'm less likely to get the animal-tested medicine. Ultimately, all of us have to do the best we can. Nothing is 100% perfect, but doing the best you can is better than doing nothing at all.

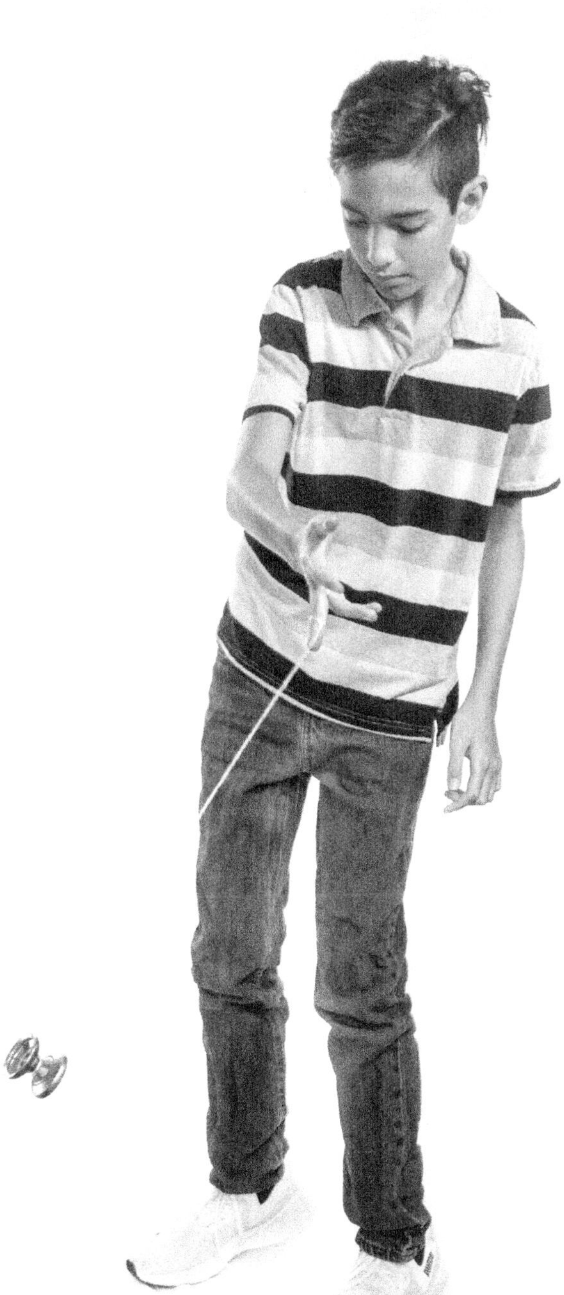

35

Attack:

Veganism is expensive.

Comeback:

What? Not at all. Besides, if you decide to stop eating animal products, you will have plenty of money for fruits and vegetables.

Explanation:

Vegan is not expensive at all. I find that meat and dairy products are more expensive in the supermarket. If you stop buying animal products, you will definitely find more cash in your wallet that you can put toward fruits and vegetables. Some things like grains and beans are very cheap for bulk amounts. A research study found that vegan meals are typically 40% cheaper than meat and fish.[20] In restaurants, it just depends on which one you're going to. Some price the vegan meal higher, and some price them lower.[20]

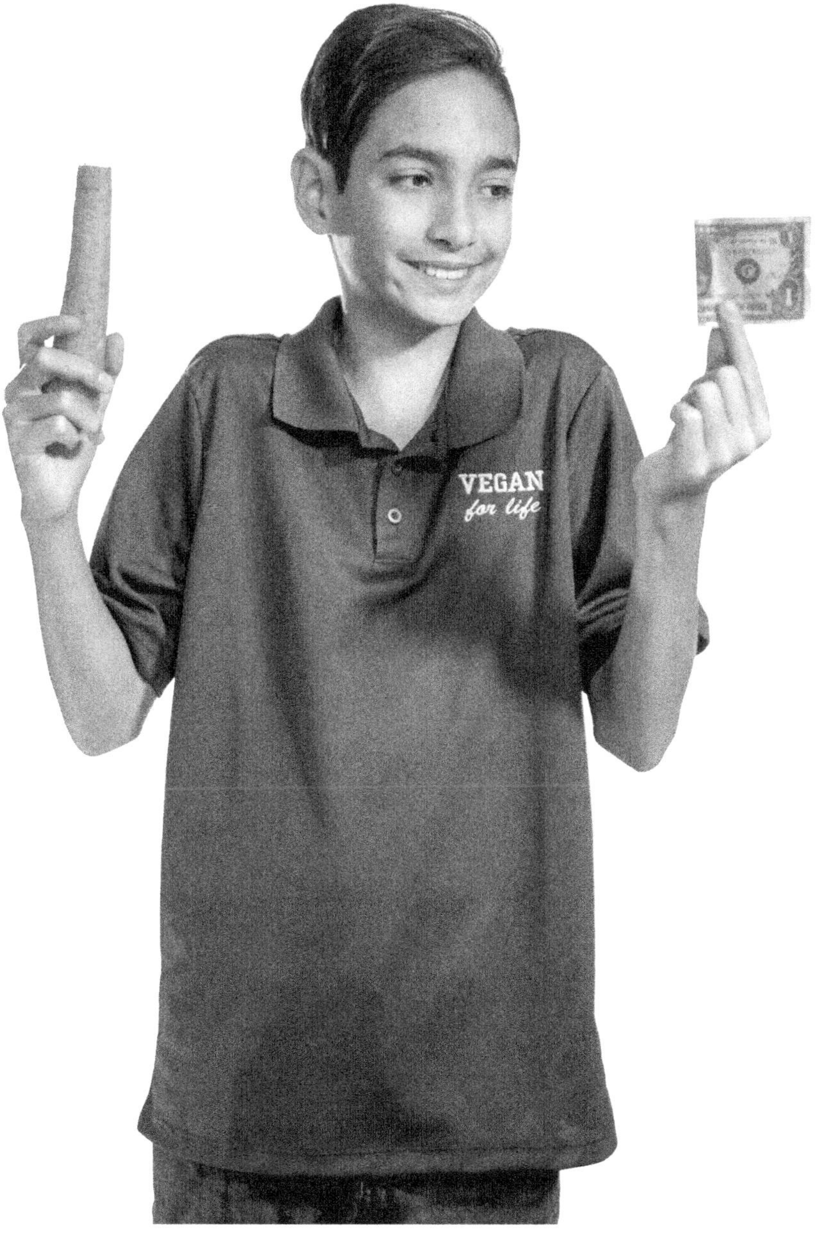
VEGAN
for life

36

Attack:

Where do you get vitamin D?

Comeback:

Same place you get it, the sun.

Explanation:

At some point, when you use one of these comebacks on a kid, they will go home crying that they lost an argument and go surfing the web to find out what veganism lacks. Eventually, they'll discover that fruits and vegetables don't provide vitamin D. What they don't realize is that food, in general, doesn't provide vitamin D and it actually comes from the Sun. [21] The dairy industry does add vitamin D to milk products, but you can take a vitamin D supplement without the milk!

85

37

Attack:

But I would never hurt an animal, I'm making use of already dead animals.

Comeback:

When you buy meat, you are paying people to kill animals.

Explanation:

Paying the people who killed an animal is the equivalent of hurting one. Imagine you find a puppy. You realize that the puppy would make a nice purse, but you hire someone to kill it rather than kill the puppy yourself since you're kind. Animal killing will stop if you stop paying and benefitting from the killers.

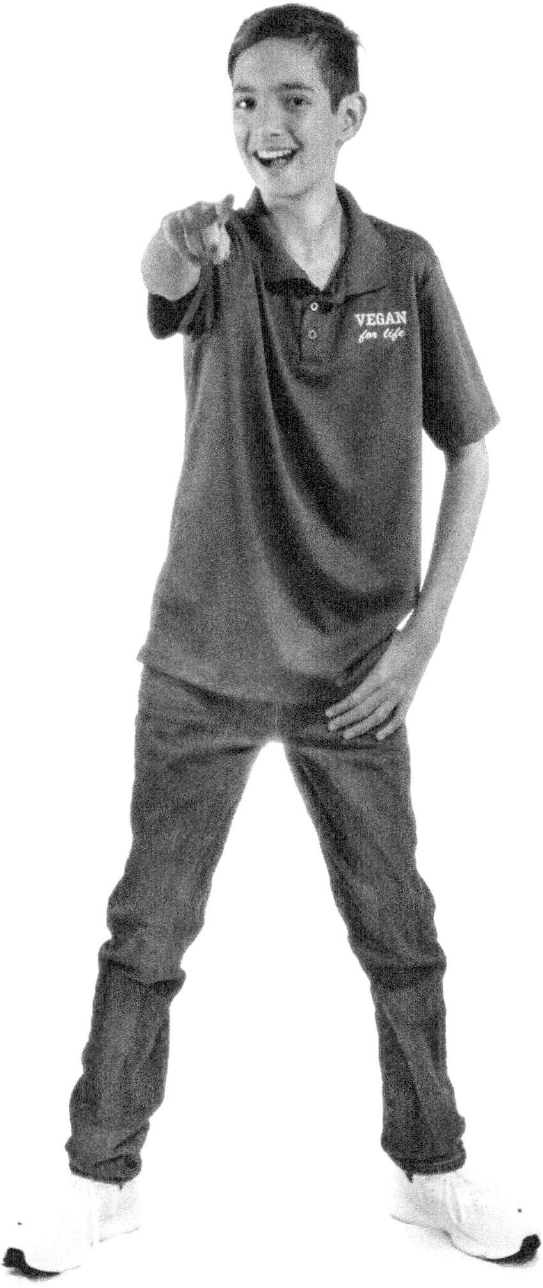
VEGAN
for life

38

Attack:

Lions can eat meat, then what's stopping us?

Comeback:

We aren't lions. (Insert optional eye roll).

Explanation:

It's apparently a little-known fact that we are humans (I've seen many people mess this up), and humans in their natural habitat are naturally vegan.[16, 28] Humans are not lions. If we were lions, we would be able to easily kill an animal with our own two hands and be able to eat the animal raw without getting sick.[16]

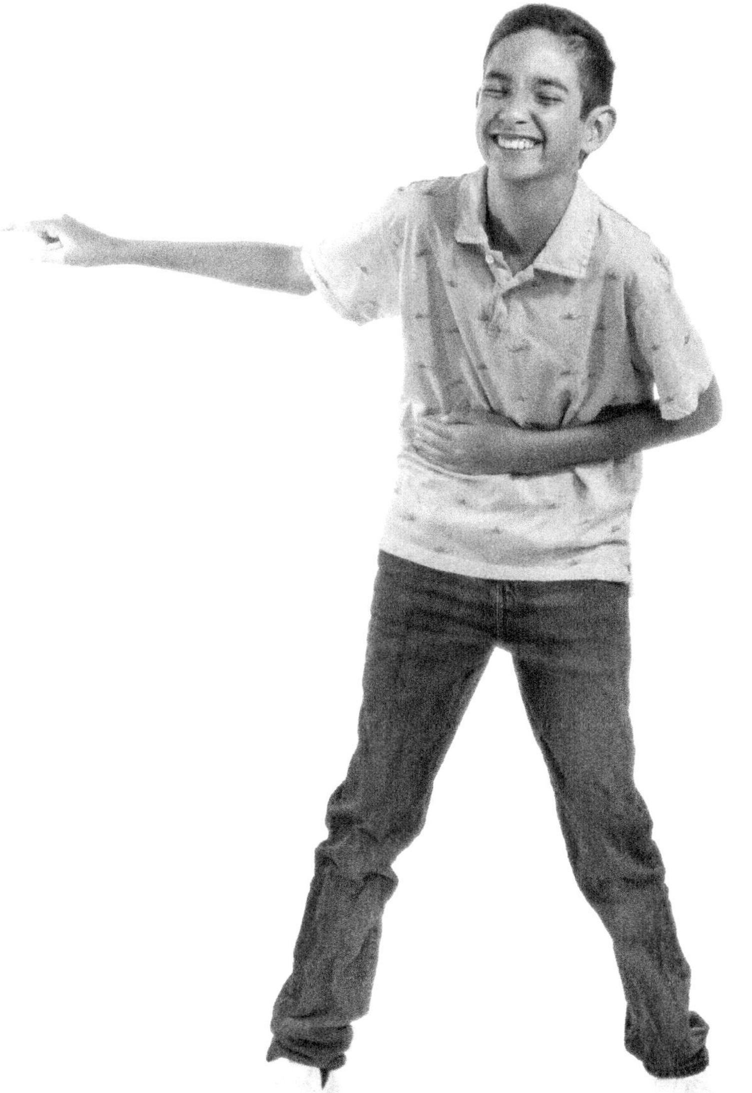

39

Attack:

Killing them humanely is okay.

Comeback:

When is any killing ever humane?

Explanation:

The dictionary defines humane as "having or showing compassion or benevolence." [49] I don't think killing anyone is showing compassion and benevolence towards them. If someone was trying to be nice to me, I wouldn't expect them to stab and murder me. The humane thing to do is just eat from plants. It's compassionate and benevolent. Kindness is always the right thing.

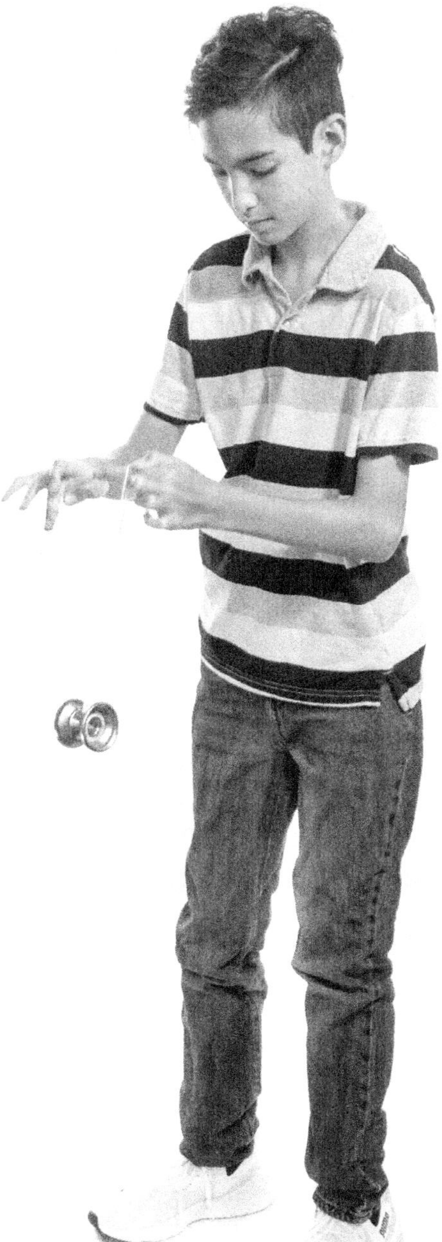

40

Attack:

What about eggs? Eggs are fine.

Comeback:

Female chickens spend their whole life in a tiny space laying eggs, and all-male chicks are ground alive because they are a waste of money. Sure, sounds totally legit.

Explanation:

It's true. Chickens live in factory farms with barely enough room to turn around! The chickens' entire life is dedicated to laying infertile eggs. That is definitely not the life the chicken wants to be living, so don't pay the people who do this. It's like making a prison for only innocent people. Everyone wants to be out and everyone deserves to be out. Just do the right thing and avoid eggs. They're just as cruel to chickens as to other animals.[22]

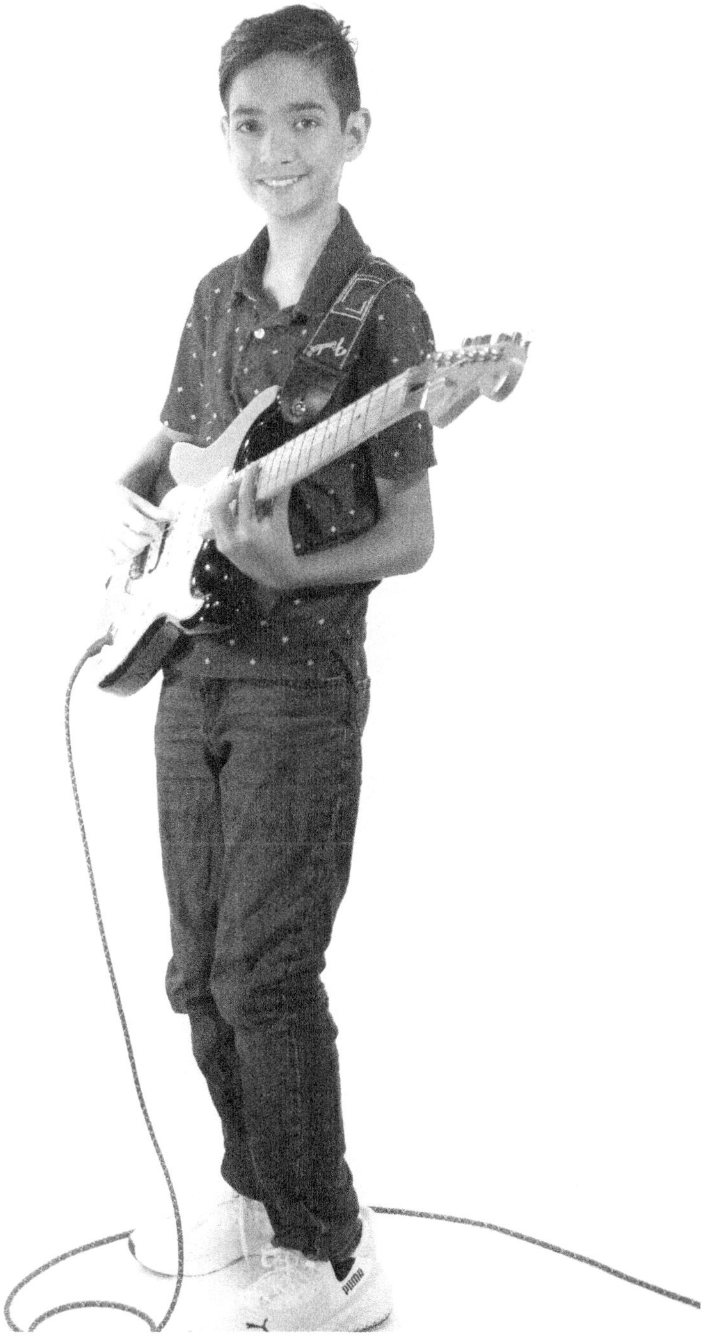
PUMA

41

Attack:

You can't be 100% vegan.

Comeback:

I'm not trying to be perfect, I'm trying to make the world a better place.

Explanation:

If you didn't understand that bit, it's impossible to be one hundred percent vegan. That would mean never hurting a bug, never eating a single animal product, even by accident (it happens), and never hurting an animal. Accidents happen. You might accidentally eat something you were told was vegan and it wasn't. Sometimes you accidentally kill a bug. As long as you put in the effort, you're vegan. It's better to try your best and not be perfect, than to not try at all. This attack is just laziness.

95

42

Attack:

But I don't want to change, I am the way I am.

Comeback:

Doing the right thing is more important than your convenience.

Explanation:

For most people, convenience is the most important thing in the world. That is why kids don't like to brush their teeth. People hate doing hard things, even if they are sabotaging themselves by doing so. Sometimes, you just have to do the right thing rather than the easier thing. The easy thing is to keep your food addictions, kill innocent animals, and continue to harm yourself with food. The right thing to do is to go vegan. Once you get used to it, it's just food and doesn't take any effort at all.

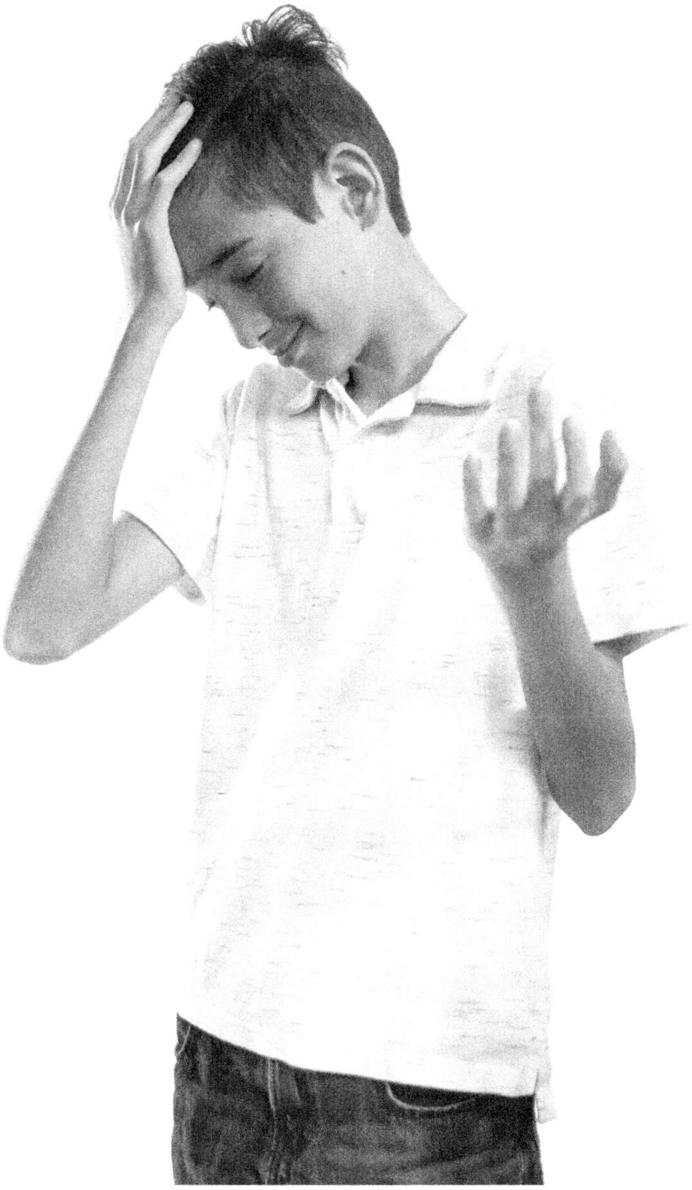

43

Attack:

But I saw on YouTube that the oldest living person eats eggs and bacon for breakfast.

Comeback:

First of all, that isn't true. But, sometimes there is a mutant that is resistant to that stuff, but if people in your family have died from high blood pressure, cancer, Lupus, or heart failure, then you probably don't have the mutant gene.

Explanation:

It happens, sometimes the oldest person is non-vegan. Sometimes a mutant gene can pass through and give people resistance against the effects of animal products. It is very rare, so don't go testing to see if you have the gene, because chances are, you're going to end up sick. In fact, there are these places called Blue Zones where the populations are mostly vegan, and people commonly live past one hundred years. A world record age would be nice, but past one-hundred is good enough for me.[23]

99

44

Attack:

Being vegan is too much of a commitment.

Comeback:

You can be vegan without an attention span.

Explanation:

Vegan is the kind of thing that you can be without thinking about it. Kind of like being able to move. You aren't constantly thinking about everything you do. For example when you read this book you don't have to think about telling your hands to hold up the book, or tell your eyes to move with the words on the page. It's just natural. When you are used to your diet, food is food. Also, I have found being kind is an instinct, it doesn't take work or focus. I think ignoring your heart to keep doing the wrong thing takes way more effort. Being vegan is a commitment, but so is not being vegan. Why not commit to doing the right thing?

H

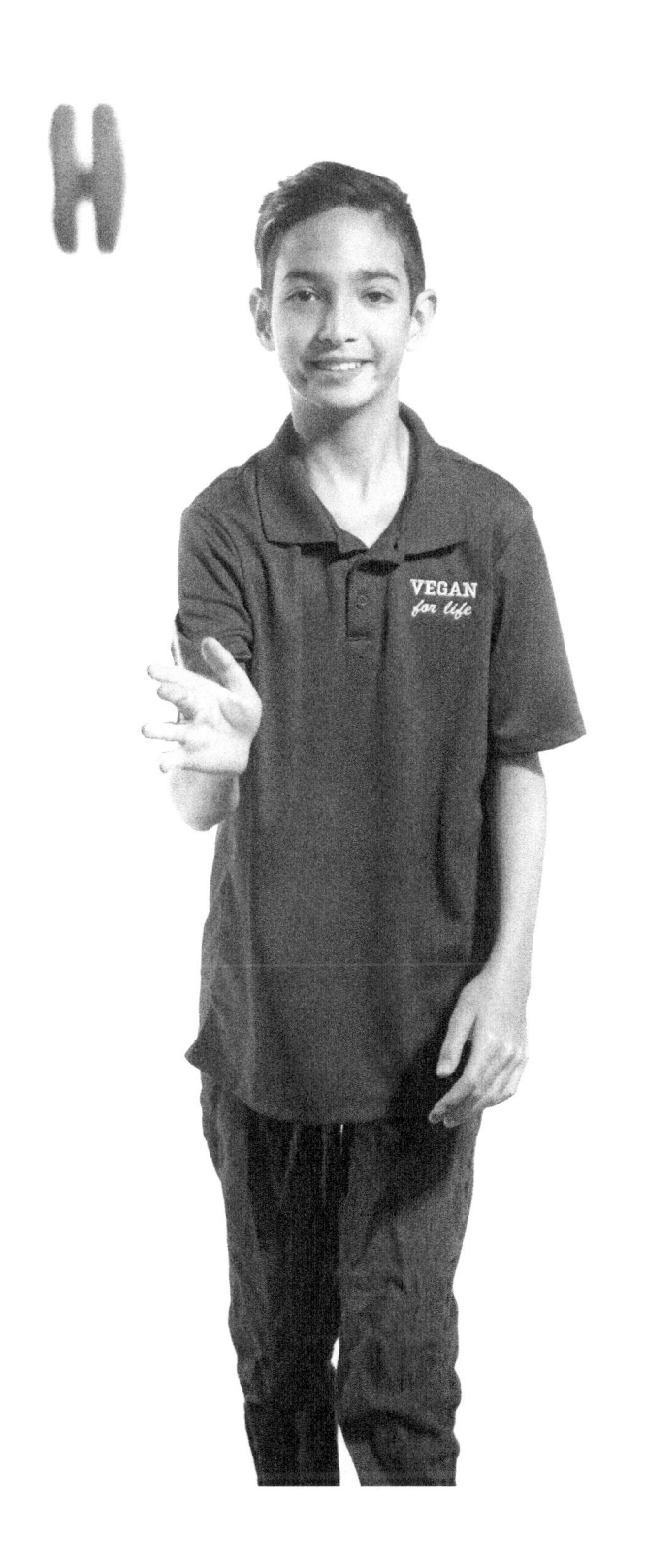

45

Attack:

Don't give me that crap, I could never give up meat.

Comeback:

Sure you could, you just have to be willing to care more about the environment, health, and animals than your own addictions.

Explanation:

The reason people don't want to give up meat and dairy products is the same reason other people don't want to give up smoking and drugs. It's all about addiction. Giving up addictions can be difficult. It takes time and effort, but eventually when you continue to stop using the thing you are addicted to, you stop craving it. Also, like drugs and smoking, animal products are deadly and will make you sick. It's just best to take the time and effort to clear the addiction because it helps you live a longer, healthier, and more ethical life, and in my opinion, that's better than short-term satisfaction.[50]

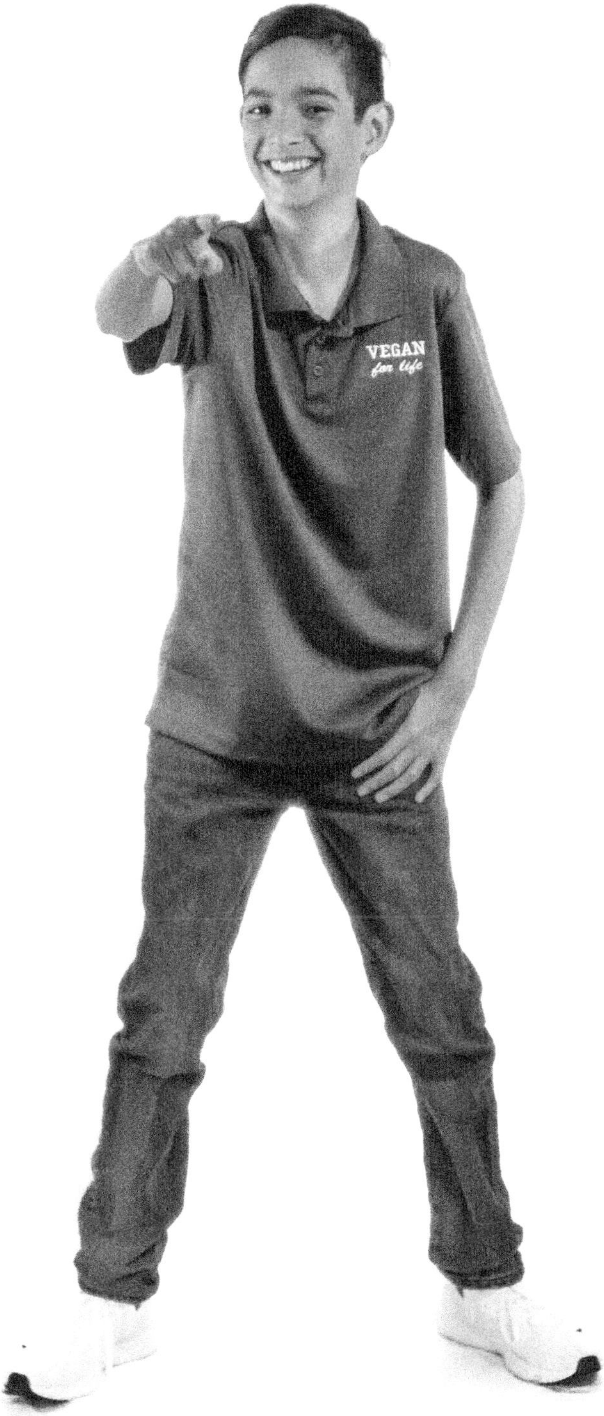
VEGAN
for life

46

Attack:

Vegan food makes you fart.

Comeback:

Meat makes you fat.

Explanation:

Veganism can make you fart more because vegetables and fruits have fiber, and when you aren't used to eating a lot of fiber, the bacteria in your gut will produce more gas as a byproduct of processing it. Research shows that over time, your gut microbiome adjusts to your new diet and you will have different beneficial bacteria that thrive on a high-fiber, plant-rich diet.[51] Also, studies have shown that fiber is important for the health of your heart and immune system.[52,53] Farts are funny. Meat and dairy products are the main cause of obesity.[13] Honestly, I prefer farting a lot over being obese. Being obese and sick is definitely worse than making the occasional fart noise.

105

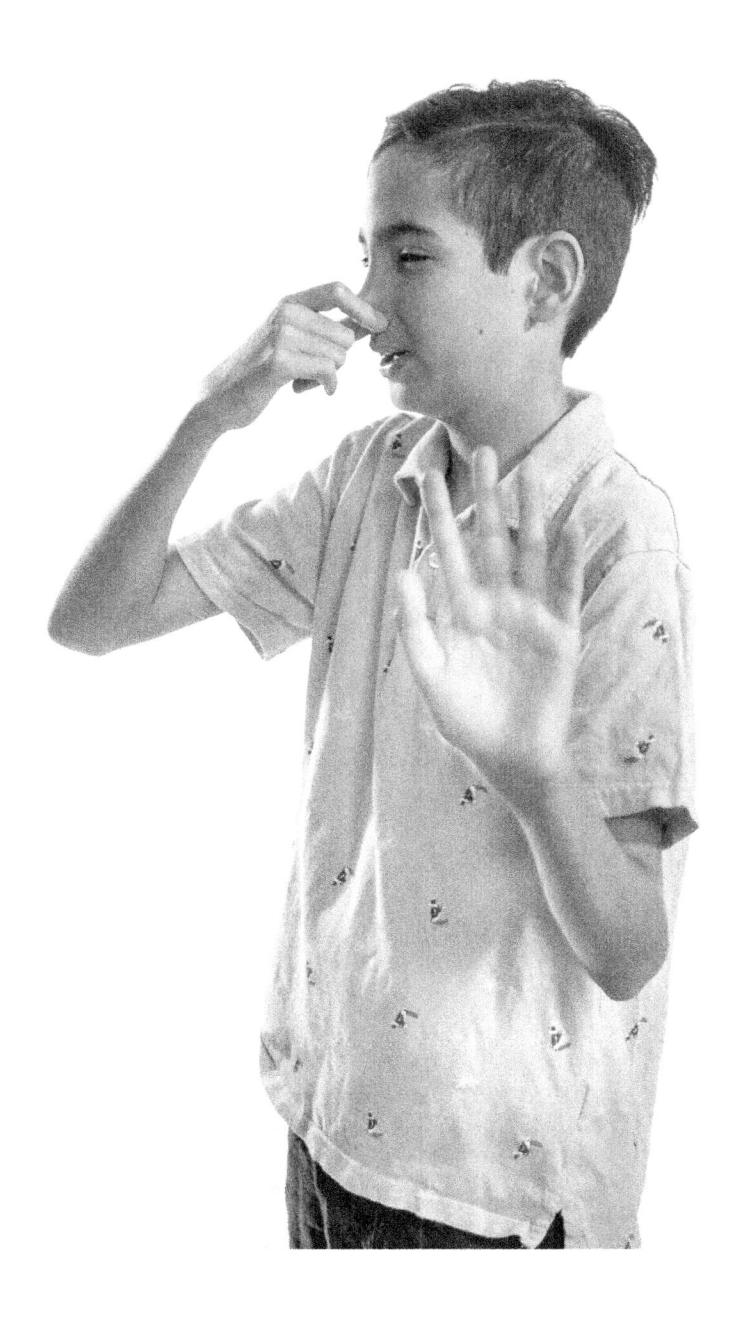

47

Attack:

I heard vegans (insert stupid lie here).

Comeback:

We are just people. Don't judge all of us by what one person says.

Explanation:

This argument is similar to saying you hate all vegan foods because you heard a story about when someone ate a rotten piece of tofu (tofu is amazing unless it's spoiled). Not everything everyone says is true, and it could apply to some. Being vegan is the kinder way of living your life, not a personality trait. It can be really annoying when someone tries to pull this. But if someone says that vegan people are smarter, that is true (there have been studies.)[54] In fact, Albert Einstein, Isaac Newton, and Leonardo Da Vinci didn't eat meat![26]

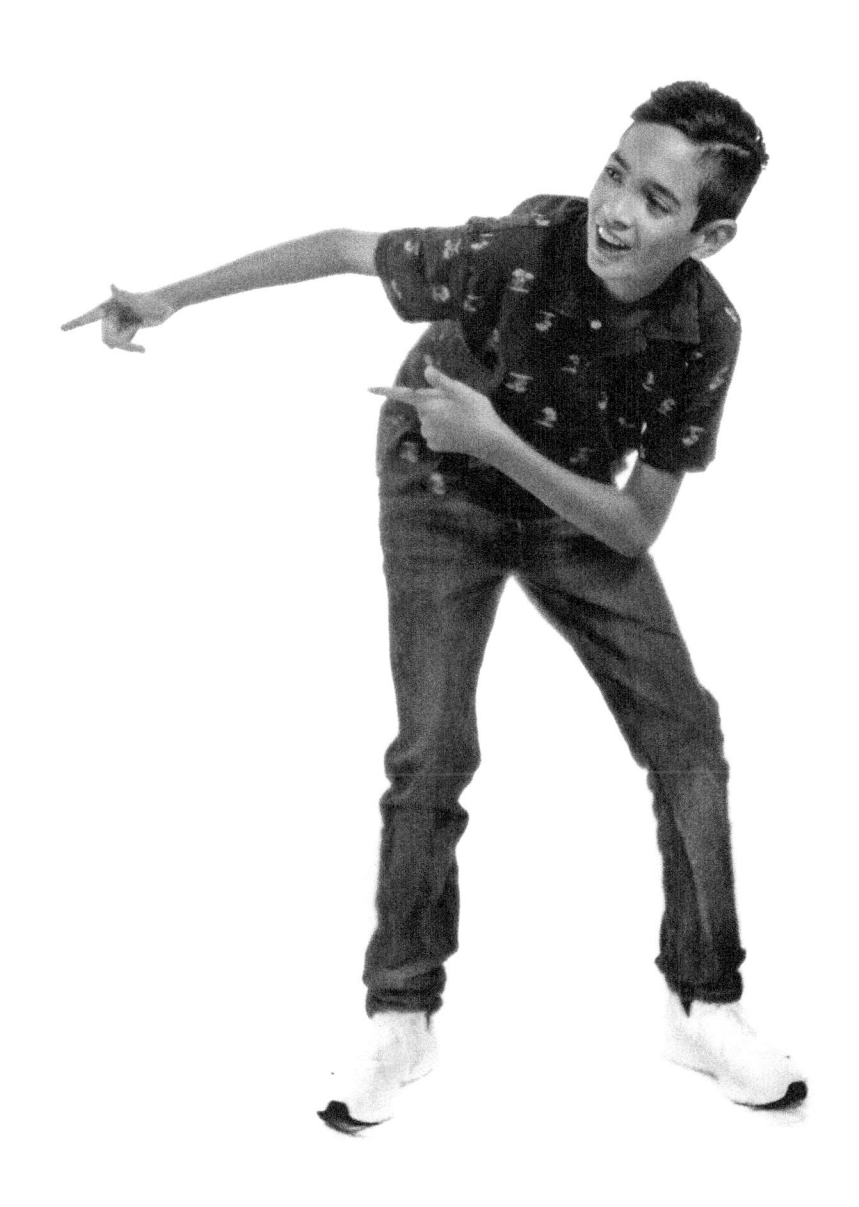

48

Attack:

But meat tastes so good!

Comeback:

Really? If you like the taste of meat, try eating it raw!

Explanation:

It's not the taste of meat that people like, they like cooked and seasoned meals that are prepared with meat. If they really liked meat, they would eat it raw and bloody, that's how real carnivores eat it. Besides, it's important to do what's right, not just what feels or tastes good. Nowadays you can eat dishes that taste like meat without the murder; you can buy vegan burgers, hot dogs, and even vegan cheeses in the supermarket and they taste great!

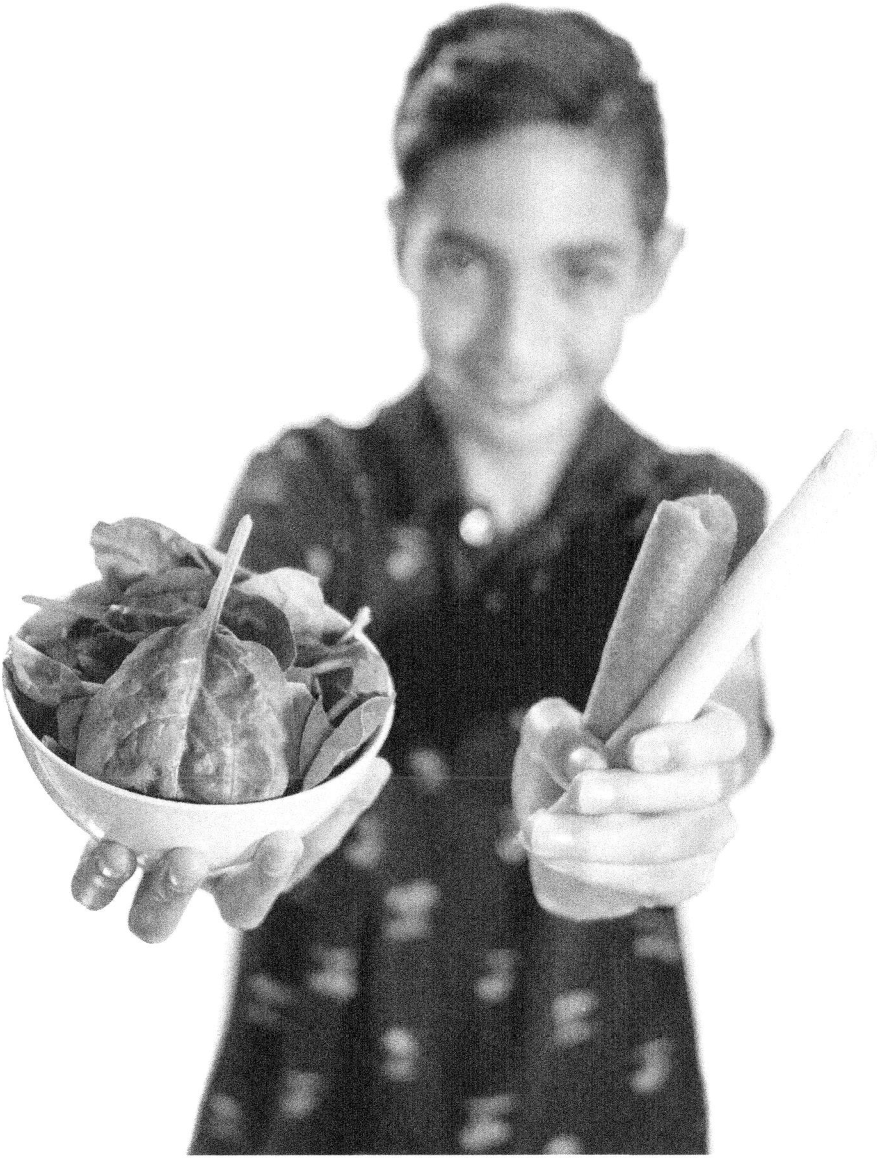

Attack:

Milk is so good! Why don't you drink it?

Comeback:

Because I'm not a baby.

Explanation:

The reason mammals produce milk is not for humans who just like the taste, it's for the animals' young. Milk is produced for babies by their mothers. Human mothers produce milk for human babies. Cows produce milk for their babies. When babies start eating regular food, they stop drinking milk. If you are reading this, I assume you aren't still drinking your mother's breast milk. Why in the world would you nurse on someone else's mother? Why would you nurse on another mammal's mother? While humans learned they could survive in times of hunger by stealing an animal's breast milk, it is not the right food for humans and it is not the right food if you aren't a baby.[27]

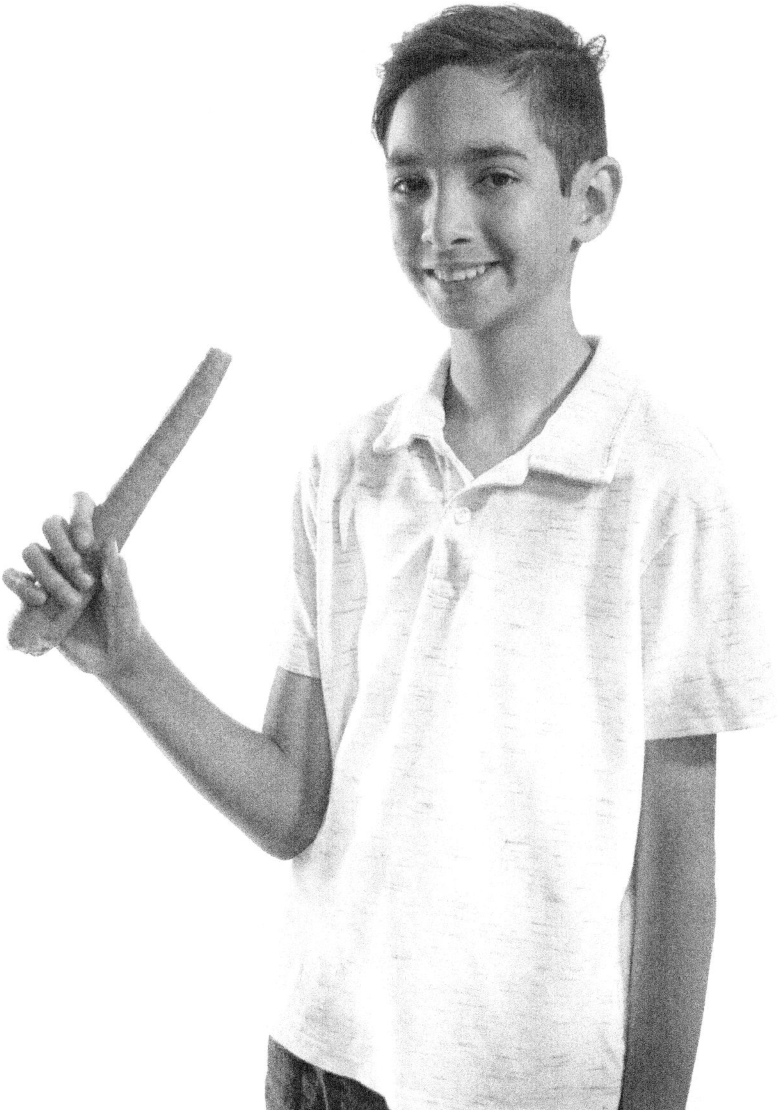

50

Attack:

I'm a carnivore!

Comeback:

No, you're a confused herbivore.

Explanation:

Humans are herbivores and there is countless evidence on the topic. First, just look at our teeth. They most resemble herbivore teeth, besides our canine teeth which are for self-defense. People also get really sick when they eat raw meat. A lion can eat a full raw animal, all the organs and the blood and be perfectly healthy. Humans are herbivores and there is no doubt about it. Maybe one person disagrees online, but if you are like most kids, your parents have probably told you not to trust everything you see online.[28] If you would rather pet a baby animal than rip it apart with your teeth and eat it, there is a good chance you are an herbivore.

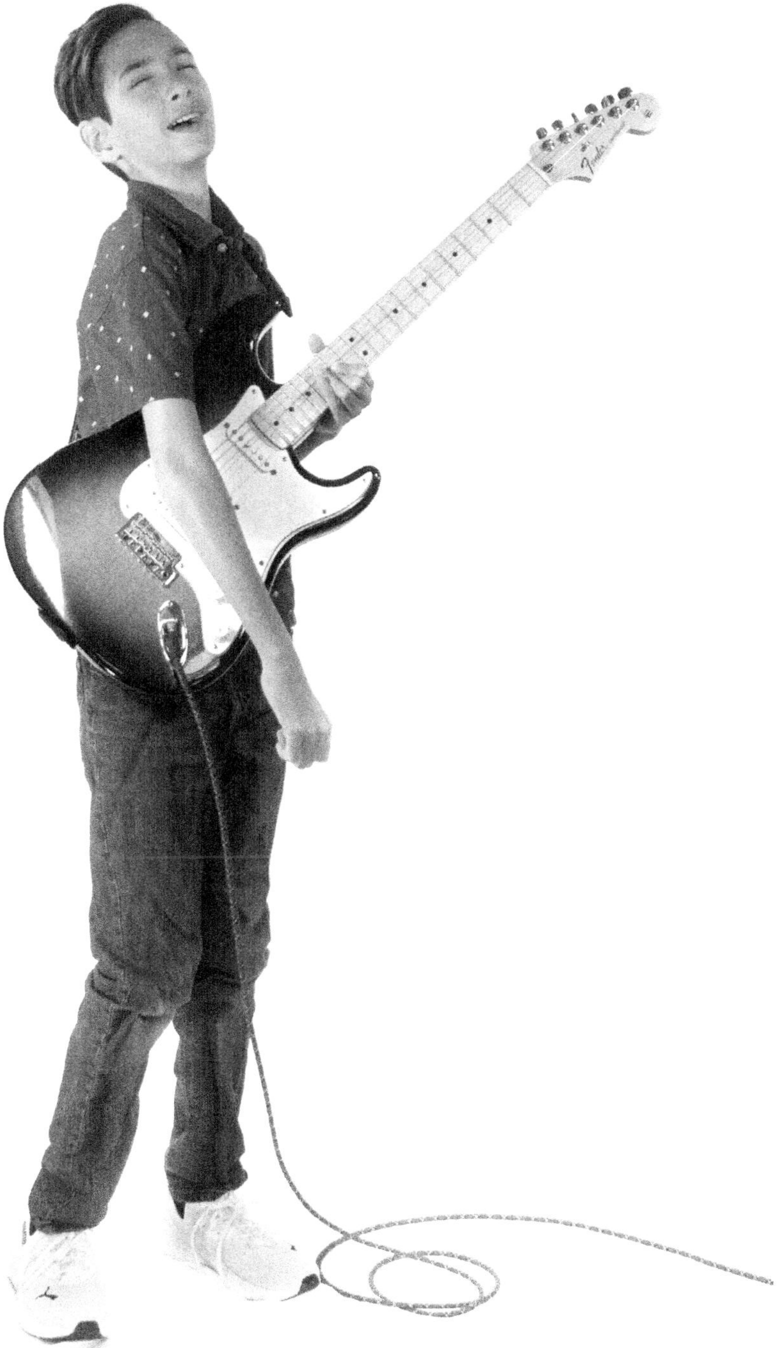

MESSAGE TO THE READER

Congratulations, you made it to the end of the book! If you didn't actually finish and you're just skipping to the end to spoil, then get back to your page and quit snooping around here!

Anyway, I hope that you can memorize a few of these comebacks and eventually build up a mental arsenal of them. Hopefully, after reading this, anyone who wants to make fun of you for being vegan will think twice about it after you hit em' with one of these comebacks.

Remember, this book is only for comebacks, not attacks. Use the knowledge in the book in response to negative things other people say, don't use it to start fights.

The best way to help the animals and the planet is to be kind to others. It's kindness that leads to conversations and open minds. Being kind does not mean letting people bully you though, so be prepared to speak up for yourself and have the deeper conversations with the people who really care enough to hear you out.

Thank you for being a part of the vegan movement. I believe one day we will have a vegan world. In the meantime, it takes every one of us to do our part, to stand up for what is right, and to stand up for ourselves and the animals. I hope this book helps you do that.

Solomon Tadlock

CITATIONS

1. Plants Neither Possess nor Require Consciousness. Lincoln Taiz et al. Trends in Plant Science, VOLUME 24, ISSUE 8, P677-687. 01-Aug- 19
2. Press Release, World Health Organization 26 October 2015
3. Eating up the world's food web and the human trophic level. Bonhommeau, Sylvain et al. PNAS. doi: 10.1073/pnas.1305827110 2-Dec-13.
4. Vitamin B 12 sources and microbial interaction. Exp Biol Med (Maywood). 2018 Jan;243(2):148-158. doi: 10.1177/1535370217746612. Epub 2017 Dec 7
5. How Safe Is Your Ground Beef? Rock, Andrea. Consumer Reports, October 2015
6. "Human Ancestors Were Nearly All Vegetarians". Rob Dunn. Sci Amer. July 23, 2012 https://blogs.scientificamerican.com/guest-blog/human-ancestors-were-nearly-all-vegetarians/
7. Hippopotamus (H. amphibius) diet change indicates herbaceous plant encroachment following megaherbivore population collapse. Kendra L. Chritz et al. Sci Rep. 2016; 6: 32807.
8. Differentiation of teeth in an individual. Phil Myers. Animal Diversity Web. Michigan Museum of Zoology
9. Tusks and Ivory . Nothing But The Tooth. Barry K.B. Berkovitz, 2013
10. Caspari, R. and Lee, S.-H. (2006), Is human longevity a consequence of cultural change or modern biology?. Am. J. Phys. Anthropol., 129: 512-517. https://doi.org/10.1002/ajpa.20360
11. https://www.forbes.com/sites/eustaciahuen/2017/04/30/why-eating-insects-may-not-be-as-sustainable-as-it-seems/?sh=2ba5b77644c1 Eustacia Huen 2017 Why Eating Insects May Not Be As Sustainable As It Seems Forbes

12. https://www.mayoclinic.org/healthy-lifestyle/nutrition-and-healthy-eating/expert-answers/high-protein-diets/faq-20058207 Katherine Zeratsky 2020 Are high-protein diets safe for weight loss? Mayo clinic

13. https://www.motherjones.com/environment/2015/11/dairy-industry-milk-federal-dietary-guidelines/ University of Adelaide. "Meat consumption contributing to global obesity." ScienceDaily. ScienceDaily, 1 August 2016. <www.sciencedaily.com/releases/2016/08/160801093003.htm>

14. https://www.cato-unbound.org/2020/02/08/shawn-e-klein/moral-status-animal-suffering 2020 Shawn E. Klein

15. "The cruelty of catch and Release Fishing", PETA, 2015 https://www.peta.org/living/entertainment/the-cruelty-of-catch-and-release-fishing/

16. "The Truth About Humans Eating Meat", PETA 2018 https://www.peta.org/living/food/really-natural-truth-humans-eating-meat/

17. "How do animals help plant reproduction?", ScienceLine, 2012 http://scienceline.ucsb.edu/getkey.php.

18. "How the dairy industry hurts cows", Kim Johnson, 2019 https://animalequality.org/blog/2019/07/09/dairy-industry-hurts-cows/

19. "Animal Agriculture Costs More In Health Damage Than It Contributes To The Economy" Forbes https://www.forbes.com/sites/jeffmcmahon/2020/12/30/animal-agriculture-costs-more-in-health-damage-than-it-contributes-to-the-economy/

20. "Research finds vegan meals 40% cheaper than meat and fish", Vegan Food and Living, 2020https://www.veganfoodandliving.com/news/research-finds-vegan-meals-cheaper-than-meat-and-fish

21. "How to Safely Get Vitamin D From Sunlight", Healthline, https://www.healthline.com/nutrition/vitamin-d-from-sun#time-of-day

22. "The species chickens", farm sanctuary, https://www.farmsanctuary.org/chickens/
23. "7 blue zone foods to include in your diet", Cathay Wong, 2020, https://www.verywellhealth.com/blue-zone-diet-foods-4159314
24. "Animals Used For Free Range Meat", PETA. https://www.peta.org/issues/animals-used-for-food/organic-free-range-meat/
25. "Obesity and weight gain", Viva, https://viva.org.uk/health/why-animal-products-harm/meat-the-truth/obesity-and-weight-gain/
26. "Eminent Scientists and Inventors on Vegetarianism", Florida News group, http://www.godsdirectcontact.org/eng/news/160/vg5.htm
27. "Why did some animals evolve breastfeeding and milk?" Shreya Dasgupta 2015 http://www.bbc.com/earth/story/20150725-breastfeeding-has-ancient-origins
28. "Humans are Herbivores", Haily Stewart 2018, https://www.uiargonaut.com/2018/11/09/humans-are-herbivores/
30. University of Adelaide. "Meat consumption contributing to global obesity." ScienceDaily. ScienceDaily, 1 August 2016. <www.sciencedaily.com/releases/2016/08/160801093003.htm>. https://www.sciencedaily.com/releases/2016/08/160801093003.htm
31. Robinson, J., Rowan, J., Campisano, C. et al. Late Pliocene environmental change during the transition from Australopithecus to Homo. Nat Ecol Evol 1, 0159 (2017). https://doi.org/10.1038/s41559-017-0159
32. Esselstyn, Caldwell, Prevent & Reverse Heart Disease. 2007
33. Campbell, T. Colin, The China Study, 2004
34. Goldner Brooke, Goodbye Lupus. 2015
35. Goldner, Brooke, Goodbye Autoimmune Disease 2019
36. 2019 "Eating red meat daily triples heart disease-related chemical" https://www.nih.gov/news-events/nih-research-

matters/eating-red-meat-daily-triples-heart-disease-related-chemical

37. Allen Press Publishing Services. "World's largest herbivore, the African elephant, makes unique food choices." ScienceDaily. ScienceDaily, 10 July 2012. <www.sciencedaily.com/releases/2012/07/120710115851.htm>.

38. "African Bush Elephant, Facts about the African elephant and how we're helping to protect them" The Nature Conservancy, July 16, 2020. https://www.nature.org/en-us/get-involved/how-to-help/animals-we-protect/african-bush-elephant/

39. The National Wildlife Federation: Polar Bears. https://www.nwf.org/Educational-Resources/Wildlife-Guide/Mammals/Polar-Bear

40. Tadlock, Thomas, Miracle Metabolism, 2017

41. "Great Vegan Athletes: Patrik Baboumian" https://www.greatveganathletes.com/patrik-baboumian-vegan-strongman/

42. "Vegan Athlete Wins Major World Bodybuilding Championship" , Plant Based News, 2019. https://plantbasednews.org/culture/vegan-wins-major-world-bodybuilding-championship/

43. Feskanich D, Willett WC, Stampfer MJ, Colditz GA. Milk, dietary calcium, and bone fractures in women: a 12-year prospective study. Am J Public Health. 1997 Jun;87(6):992-7. doi: 10.2105/ajph.87.6.992. PMID: 9224182; PMCID: PMC1380936.

44. Frank, J. An Interactive Model of Human and Companion Animal Dynamics: The Ecology and Economics of Dog Overpopulation and the Human Costs of Addressing the Problem. Human Ecology 32, 107–130 (2004). https://doi.org/10.1023/B:HUEC.0000015213.66094.06

45. "What is the difference between veganism and vegetarianism?" Jamie Eske, 2019, https://www.medicalnewstoday.com/articles/325478

46. "Humans Are Natural Vegetarians" Huffington Post Kathy Freston, Nov 17, 2011. https://www.huffpost.com/entry/shattering-the-meat-myth_b_214390

47. Holy Bible. King James Version Gen 1:29

48. "Strange Noises turn out to be cows missing their calves", Dave Rogers, 2013, https://www.newburyportnews.com/news/local_news/strange-noises-turn-out-to-be-cows-missing-their-calves/article_d872e4da-b318-5e90-870e-51266f8eea7f.html

49. "Humane", The Oxford Dictionary https://www.lexico.com/en/definition/humane http://ahimsaacres.org/Dale/May-2017/The_Truth_About_Meat_and_Dairy_Addiction_(Dale).pdf

50. Barnard, Neal, M.D., Breaking the Food Seduction, St. Martin's Griffin, 2003

51. Kahleova H, Fleeman R, Hlozkova A, Holubkov R, Barnard ND. A plant-based diet in overweight individuals in a 16-week randomized clinical trial: metabolic benefits of plant protein. Nutr Diabetes. 2018;8(1):58. Published 2018 Nov 2. doi:10.1038/s41387-018-0067-4

52. Daniel F.Zegarra-Ruiz12AsmaaEl Beidaq1Alonso J.Iñiguez13MartinaLubrano Di Ricco14SilvioManfredo Vieira1William E.Ruff1DerekMubiru1Rebecca L.Fine1JohnSterpka1Teri M.Greiling15CarinaDehner1Martin A.Kriegel. A Diet-Sensitive Commensal Lactobacillus Strain Mediates TLR7-Dependent Systemic Autoimmunity Cell Host & Microbe. Volume 25, Issue 1, 9 January 2019, Pages 113-127.e6

53. Pereira MA, O'Reilly E, Augustsson K, et al. Dietary Fiber and Risk of Coronary Heart Disease: A Pooled Analysis of Cohort Studies. Arch Intern Med. 2004;164(4):370–376. doi:10.1001/archinte.164.4.370

54. Gale CR, Deary IJ, Schoon I, Batty GD. IQ in childhood and vegetarianism in adulthood: 1970 British cohort study. BMJ. 2007;334(7587):245. doi:10.1136/bmj.39030.675069.55

Printed in Great Britain
by Amazon